THE ART AND SKILL OF
SALES
PSYCH?L!GY

THE ART AND SKILL OF
SALES
PSYCHOLOGY

*Why Buyers and Sellers
Do What They Do*

BRAD McDONALD

Foreword by **David Mattson**

Paperback: 978-0-578-46727-6

E-book: 978-0-578-46728-3

Contents

To my father,
Ewing Raiford "Mickey" McDonald Jr.—
the original Captain McDonald.

Acknowledgments

For encouraging me to hang in there during the rough seas of my early sales days, I send special thanks to my wife Kim, as well as all our family: Tyler, Luke, Mary, Rose, Ava, Colin, Ewing, and Bailey.

Also, thanks to my mother for proofing and editing all of my articles. Thanks to my dad who always believed I could move the world with my fingertips. I'm not that good, but he thought I was. You're forever in my heart, Dad.

FOREWORD

As I was reading Brad McDonald's fine book, I was reminded of one of the selling rules formulated by the founder of our company, David Sandler. It's one that sometimes stops people in their tracks when they hear it for the first time. The rule is: "Selling is a Broadway show performed by a psychiatrist."

Many people hear that and ask themselves what the statement could possibly mean—and whether it's really a rule at all. Here's a brief overview of what Sandler was getting at. First, the reference to the Broadway show, which puzzles a lot of people, is meant to remind salespeople that selling is a performance. That means you're playing a role, and you know it. You might sometimes do things a little differently than you would otherwise do them based on the situation you're facing and the requirements of the role you're playing. You might on occasion act as though you don't know something that you actually do know. You might choose to speak slowly and methodically to someone who needs that kind of pacing, when your initial instinct might be to speak quickly and with enthusiasm. You understand that you're giving a performance, and you tailor that performance to the situation you face and the audience that's in front of you.

What about the "performed by a psychiatrist" part of this rule? What Sandler was trying to remind salespeople about is the inescapable reality that to be successful, you need to develop a deep understanding of the human dynamics that underlie any and every selling situation. You need to be able to manage your communication and your own emotions based on fundamental principles of human behavior—principles that many salespeople overlook or never study.

Brad's book is, for salespeople, an in-depth, and long-overdue, examination of the neglected art of putting on that Broadway play and the equally neglected doing so as a psychiatrist—or, at least, as a layman with a basic understanding of the important psychological principles that can influence the selling cycle. The book also gives managers some important insights and strategies on understanding the human dynamics of their working relationships with the salespeople who report to them. It's an important resource—one that I think every sales professional should read.

David Mattson
President/CEO, Sandler Training

Introduction

·······························

Sales is an emotionally charged vocation. Sometimes all it takes is one unsuccessful appointment, one prospect who looked hopeful and then went dark, or one too many think-it-overs to cause a salesperson to question their choice of profession—or judgment.

My own initial foray into sales, after a long, proud career in the United States Navy, had more than its share of emotional ups and downs. A little background: I followed in my father's footsteps to become a submarine captain. I worked on five different submarines and served as commanding officer on the fifth. I was leading security operations in the Mediterranean and the Atlantic and supporting classified missions that involved a Navy SEAL team. I was in charge, and I was comfortable with that. When I said, "Jump," people asked, "How high?" I was a valiant and brave sailor on the high seas. I faced death on a regular basis. Yet when I transitioned into civilian life and started making sales calls, I didn't feel so brave. Why was I terrified to pick up the phone and make a cold call?

I realized I had entered a whole new world. Prospects thought nothing of misleading, obfuscating, or out-and-out lying to me about their intentions. Typically, they ignored my requests or suggestions. My sales interactions often felt more like fights than mutually beneficial engagements for both parties.

My big learning point came with the discovery of Sandler Training and the help of my beloved sales mentor, Coach Jim Rohrbach. He helped me figure out that sales was as much a mind game as anything. Prospects, Jim told me, would play with my mind just as much as I let them.

Sun Tzu, an ancient-Chinese general and military strategist, said, "If you know the enemy and know yourself, you need not fear the results of a hundred battles." My parallel became, "If I know my prospects and know myself, I need not fear the results of a hundred sales calls."

My efforts at learning led me to sit down every Sunday afternoon for several years to write an article on what I had learned about the sales process. This book is a compilation of some of these articles. When I looked back at the collection, I realized that it is all psychology. I'm no psychologist, for sure, but if I were starting in sales today, I would first run to the nearest bookstore for books on psychology and concern myself with sales tactics later.

If you are in sales and have struggled to understand the mind of your prospect; if you wonder why honest, moral, ethical people think they can lie to a salesperson and still make it to heaven; if you want to better control that sales interaction that seems to ride a fine line between trust and confusion; or if you struggle to understand your own mindset and frustrations when selling—perhaps this book will speak to you and provide an insight or two that will help you in controlling your sales calls.

To sales managers and coaches, let me suggest that the best way to help your struggling salesperson may be to help them create a better understanding of people's fears, anxieties, and confusion about the sales process—both the seller's and the buyer's. If you're willing to consider that possibility, please think of this book as a primer for exploring why people do what they do in sales situations. Understanding this is more essential than drilling your team in the right tactics. Of course, the tactics are important. They're the answer to the question, "What do I do?" But understanding the *why* behind that *what* might be the best place to start.

Most salespeople genuinely want to do good things for their prospects and clients; they also want to make a living, prosper, and eliminate the frustration of negative sales interactions. Here's to doing those good things, making a decent living, prospering, and pursuing a frustration-free sales career.

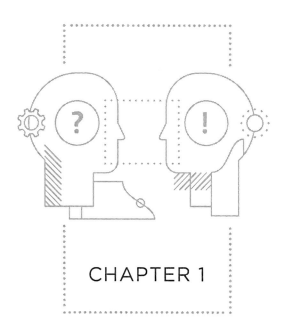

CHAPTER 1

Eleven Advantages of a Selling Career

C omedian Rodney Dangerfield built his career on a signature tag line: "I get no respect." Unfortunately, there are far too many salespeople who suffer from the Dangerfield syndrome. Either they feel they get no respect or, worse, they act that way. They walk around with sullen expressions and a woe-is-me outlook. They are selling sympathy rather than solutions. If this is describing you, study this carefully. Hold your head high and display the pride of your profession. Selling is a great field. It has advantages that few other careers can claim.

1. **Selling solves problems and fulfills needs.**

   What you're selling will either relieve pain or provide pleasure. Depending on what you sell, customers will be better able to solve problems, make more money, serve others better, enhance their self-esteem, improve their knowledge, or fulfill a heart's desire. When you do your job, you help people get what they want out of life.

2. **Only your efforts and creativity limit your potential.**

   Selling is the classic example of pay-for-performance. This explains why so many high-energy, focused people are attracted to sales. Their level of achievement—and their income—has no ceiling.

3. **Selling provides an opportunity to work with people.**

   Are people exasperating? Absolutely. Will they give you heartaches, headaches, and stomachaches? Without question. But they are also fun, exciting, and challenging. As a salesperson, you experience this exhilarating challenge every time you go to work.

4. **Selling may be the purest form of empowerment.**

   When you sell, you have to solve problems on the spot. You are accountable for solving a customer's problem then and there. While everyone else in your company may be debating the pros and cons of empowerment, you are living it.

5. **Selling is a psychological high.**

   Many workers finishing an eight-hour shift are not relishing their next chance to return to the assembly line. But look at any salesperson who has just closed an important deal, landed a new customer, or solved a current customer's problem. You're watching a winner.

6. **Selling makes you test your mettle every day.**

   Every time athletes step onto the playing field, they have to prove themselves. They're only as good as their next performance. Sales provides you the same opportunity to show your stuff.

7. **Selling provides immediate feedback on your performance. It's also unmistakable.**

   The reactions you get from buyers and customers leave no doubt of how you're doing. You can use that feedback to constantly improve. Every time you present yourself and your product, you have a chance to sharpen your skills.

8. **Selling generates revenue—the lifeblood of a company.**

   A company makes money only when a customer decides to buy its product. You help the customer make that decision. As long as you're generating sales, you have little reason to worry about job security.

9. **Selling is the direct communication link between the customer and the company.**

   Salespeople are in the best position to monitor market trends. Your customers tell you exactly what's right and wrong with your product, what to improve, and what to leave alone. You hear about their pains and frustrations, and you hear about their dreams and aspirations. You are the eyes and ears of the company.

10. **Selling provides a path for upward mobility.**

    Sales is a highly visible office in most companies. When you succeed, everyone in your company as well as your competitors know it. Your chance for advancement increases in direct proportion to your sales success.

11. **Sales prepares you for other careers.**

    The on-the-job training you get in sales is unparalleled. You succeed in sales only by being an effective presenter, psychologist, sociologist, planner, peacemaker, negotiator, consultant, leader, follower, financier, and deliverer.

    Don't get NO R-E-S-P-E-C-T? Try selling. The best salespeople have the most self-respect of all. They know they've mastered the toughest job on the planet.

CHAPTER 2

The Right Stuff
for Selling

S o, you want to go into sales.

Real estate, autos, mortgage, financial services, insurance, heating and cooling, swimming pools, roofing, home improvements, computer software, IT services—the list of things you can sell to make a living goes on and on.

On top of that is another endless list. This is the list of network marketing programs, each of which holds out the possibility of making a budding entrepreneur flush with success and cash.

Most companies survive on sales. One major company has more than a hundred sales representatives combing my local area every day, servicing existing accounts and endeavoring to open new accounts. Professional selling offers an abundance of career opportunities. There is never a shortage of available sales positions. If you can sell well, companies will line up to hire you.

Hundreds, possibly thousands, of people enthusiastically start some type of sales career in my area alone every year. Yet, a great many of those people lose their steam, get discouraged, get scared, give up, and wash out of sales jobs in their first year. One auto dealership owner told me he had 80 salespeople come and go one year—ouch! That's a lot of time and effort wasted on people who didn't work out. Want to go into sales? Make sure you have the right stuff.

What is the right stuff? There are many behavioral traits that I look for when assessing potential new hires for sales positions. Here are the top five.

1. **Goal Orientation**—Ambition and desire to be the best.

   Nobody can instill this in you; either you have it or you don't. If you don't, then you will give up too easily when your new sales job gets hard (and it will). A person with strong goal orientation wants to be the best, consistently sets more demanding goals, and is ambitious. Most people come into sales with aspirations of great success and a huge income, but as soon as they achieve an income that puts them in their comfort zone, they throttle back and do only what is necessary to maintain their status quo.

2. **Initiative**—Taking action without being told.

Sales can be a very independent job. The thing I like best about my job is that nobody tells me what to do. But that can be a problem, too—if you need somebody to tell you what to do, then sales is not the place for you.

3. **Ego**—Gaining respect and demonstrating confidence.

If your ego drive is low, then you're dealing with two problems. One is that you're not driven internally to satisfy a level of sales success and don't get the high that top-notch sales professionals get from closing a deal. The second is that a weak ego may mean a weak self-image, and the constant rejection and disregard by prospects will tear you up emotionally. A high ego drive will motivate you to be constantly looking for your next sale and also protect your self-image against the emotional roller-coaster of sales.

4. **Vitality**—Maintaining energy and stamina.

People low in vitality do not have the stamina to prospect on an ongoing basis. Sales success does not require 14-hour days but it does require an unrelenting approach to looking for and qualifying prospects.

5. **Time Competency**—Managing time effectively.

Probably half of all salespeople I speak with mention time management as one of their biggest problems. The real problem is usually making the right choices. Most people, given the choice between visiting existing clients (who will be happy to see you) and seeking out new prospects (who will not be happy to see you) will usually find time for the former and not the latter. The choice here should be a no-brainer.

The traits listed above are just part of a total assessment, and everyone thinks they have them. But if you're contemplating a career in sales, make sure you measure up in these five areas. If you're a business owner or sales manager, look carefully at your prospective hires in light of these traits.

With all the available tools for assessing job candidates, most sales managers and owners still hire based on three things: a resume, an interview, and a reference from a previous employer. But have you ever seen a resume that indicated anything less than a super hero? Have you ever interviewed someone who said, "I'm an average performer"? Have you ever given out a reference that would give you anything less than an A+?

Remember the person you are hiring is no more the person you interviewed than the person you married was the person you dated. If you want to find out how a candidate will perform after the honeymoon is over, consider using an online assessment tool, such as the Extended DISC Profile (www.extendeddisc.org) or the Devine Inventory (www.devinegroup.com), both of which are available through your local Sandler® trainer (www.sandler.com). These assessments will tell you what lies beyond the resume and interview and specifically what you can expect in the areas discussed above.

People looking for a job always put their best foot forward, as they should. But that is just the beginning. If, as a manager, you like what you see in a prospective salesperson, then assess and verify to get beneath the charming exterior and find out if they have the right stuff to sell well.

CHAPTER 3

Sit Back, Relax, and Enjoy the Cold Call

I t's the first and last topic covered at flight attendant and commercial pilot training.

"Make sure you tell those miserable people, stuffed in their undersized seats like sardines, with their knees in their chests, inside a noisy aluminum tube, to 'Sit back, relax, and enjoy the flight.'"

How can I possibly enjoy it? It's uncomfortable, confining, and loud. Flying is to my life as prospecting is to my sales—a necessary but unpleasant duty. But if I am going to visit faraway friends and family, attend important conferences, and—most importantly—see my grandchildren, then flying is a necessity.

If I want new clients to replace those who will inevitably depart, if I want to grow my business, or if I just want to stay in business, prospecting is not optional.

Why pick a profession with such a negative side? Possibly because I couldn't think of any other profession that doesn't have some painful aspect to it. Once I made peace with the difficult aspects of sales and decided to stay, I realized time would have to be spent prospecting.

If you love picking up the phone to call 20 strangers, unannounced, knowing that 18–19 of those folks will tell you to "get lost," then read no further.

But if, like me, you would rather be home in your garage all alone doing woodwork or some other hobby, the tips below may help ease the pressure of prospecting.

- Remember that cold calling is not forever. Many of us must start with a lot of cold calls and walk-ins. But after a few years the referrals grow. Once in a while, a good prospect actually calls me. I make few cold calls now, and mainly do it to test my mettle—to make sure I'm still tough enough to do it.

- Recognize that you'll probably need to make some finite number of dead-end calls before the next positive response. Each call you make will reduce that number.

- For each call you are about to make, picture your competitor sitting at a phone dialing the same number.
- Stop waiting for cold calls to be enjoyable. This is the most miserable part of sales.

Many people leave sales because they can't stand the rejection. They view it as a personal failure. However, professions like civil engineer, brain surgeon, or airline pilot are not known for rewarding even one failure. In sales, failure is a good thing. It means you are out there swinging. Iconic baseball legend Babe Ruth struck out twice as often as he hit a home run. Here are some tips for "rejecting rejection."

- Expect your share of rejection. I'm guessing the Babe did not sulk when he struck out. He knew he was that much closer to the next home run.
- Let "no" be your second favorite word. It's better than dealing with "let me think it over" or "send me some literature."
- Understand why people are mean sometimes. It usually has nothing to do with you. In that moment, they may have needed somebody to dump on, and you were the first person handy. You bravely put yourself in the line of fire and became a convenient target. Maybe you spared someone else. Move on.
- Focus on the long term. Tomorrow you'll barely

remember today's bad calls, and next week they'll be gone. In the context of life, today's rejection is no big deal.

- You don't have to turn suspects into prospects any more than a gold miner has to turn gravel into gold. You're just on a search for that which is already gold—that interested person—so you can set an appointment. If there is no interest, politely disengage. Prospecting should be a no-pressure activity for both parties.

- Avoid PAB: prospecting avoidance behavior. Anything can become more urgent than making calls when it is time to prospect. I know, I have a PhD in PAB!

Now it's time for you to stop reading. You better get back to the phone, so you can sit back, relax, and enjoy the cold call.

CHAPTER 4

Embrace Failure

Do you hear, "Let me think it over," more often than you hear "yes" or "no"? Unfortunately, the problem may be you. As I will explore in detail later (see Chapter 23), there is a very strong correlation between salespeople's own decision processes and what they will tolerate from their prospects; only decision makers can get people to make decisions. So, if you find yourself constantly facing the dreaded, "Let me think it over," you might need to take a look at how you make decisions and improve where necessary.

Being a strong and effective decision maker involves

taking risk, being open to the possibility of failure, and identifying and eliminating procrastination. As I said in the prior chapter, in sales, failure is a good thing. Failure brings profound lessons; procrastination can be avoided; and decisions can be improved by a process that involves all of these ideas. As you become more decisive, you will find that your prospects mysteriously follow suit.

Let's take a look at the anatomy of failure. Recently, I heard noted and immensely successful business consultant and author Alan Weiss speak at a conference in Richmond. One thing he said over and over in his talk was, "I'm not afraid to fail; if I'm not failing, I'm not trying." This is contrary to the theme in the greater culture of never acknowledging the possibility of failure. In my previous life, as a submarine captain, failure was not looked on with favor. One collision, one grounding, one bad incident, and you are looking for another job. In business, and particularly in sales, it's all different. You have to be willing to fail every day. You know that nine out of ten potential buyers are likely to tell you "no." You're just hoping that the tenth one will like you enough to think about buying your stuff. That's a 10% success rate— not very good by the world's standard.

When you have a significant business or personal failure, here is what ensues:

- **Disbelief.** Your mind will deny what it can't accept. "I can't believe this is happening to me." Avoid making major decisions at this point. This is not a good time to give up on your goals and dreams.

- **Fear.** After disbelief comes fear. Fear can be useful if you understand and control it; but it can be paralyzing if you exaggerate it. Fear is necessary for survival, but don't let it overwhelm or control you. Remember the words of Franklin Roosevelt: "The only thing we have to fear is fear itself."
- **Despair.** Reality returns, and despair or loss of hope comes with it. You accept what has happened but you may not accept responsibility, and you might not believe that things can ever get better.
- **Anger.** You think your world is crumbling, and you get angry. Again, this is not a time to make a major decision. As the frustration builds, you may divert the anger to a situation outside the area of failure. Be careful not to vent your anger on innocent bystanders.
- **Acceptance.** The anger subsides, and you start to accept responsibility for the failure. You realize it is time to move on.

No part of this process is fun, but it is not a reason to give up on your goals or dreams. Don't short-circuit the process; time will ease the pain. Also, you will learn many valuable lessons.

- **You learn to understand yourself.** This may be painful, but you will exhibit responsibility and learn from your failure.

- **You reorder your priorities.** You will learn a lot about what is and what is not important in your life.
- **You strengthen your "gut" system.** You have choices: either sit in the corner and mope, or get on with your life. If you choose the latter, you will learn that failure has an up-side and you will get tough and develop the guts to do what you need to do to be successful.

I'm not encouraging failure, just emphasizing the fact that failure is going to happen and that it has value as a learning tool. If you learn from failure, then it should not deter you from your long-term goals and, ultimately, it will make you stronger. Learning to deal with failure is the first step in eliminating failure from your life and your sales processes. Remember—if you're not failing, you're not trying.

CHAPTER 5

Breaking Through Your Sales Comfort Zone

A re you in sales for the long haul? Have you burned your bridges for ever going back to the secure life of a guaranteed paycheck? Or are you just in sales until the next good job offer comes along?

People don't fail in sales because of bad prospects, bad products, bad markets, or bad economic times. These are just the excuses they use. People fail in sales because they stop believing in themselves.

The most important thing you need to be successful in

sales is a strong self-image. Sales is a high-risk business. Every day you face rejection, humiliation, failure, and uncertainty. If you have a weak self-image, you may take these experiences personally. Soon you'll be reluctant to put yourself in risky situations. When that happens, it's only a matter of time before you give up on yourself and your sales career, which had, at one time, looked so promising to you.

The reason many salespeople have problems in this area is that they confuse their self-image with their roles in life. The well-known I/R (Identity/Role) Theory illuminates the dual nature of our lives. Each of us has an "I" and an "R." Our "I" represents our values, beliefs, principles, desires and emotions—our inner selves. Our "R" is made up of the many roles we play in our lives, or our outer selves. These roles include son, daughter, friend, student, salesperson, and so on. The I/R model was developed to define the relationship between those two parts of our whole and to help distinguish between them. Although they are separate, they affect each other. In order to separate the two, let's define them.

First: roles, your "R." Roles are the labels you put on yourself; they are what you do. Examples are: parent, salesperson, spouse, manager, trainer, business owner, or company president. Stop and make a list of four or five roles that you have.

Now consider this: All of these roles can be taken away from you. Pretend for a minute that you are on a deserted island for an hour and you have no roles. It's just you—no labels, no roles. How do you feel about yourself? On a scale of 1 to 10, rate your value or self-worth with no roles.

Now consider your "I," your identity. This is made up of your values, principles, and beliefs. Examples are honesty, faithfulness, reliability, charity, compassion, and stewardship. Make a list of four or five values and principles that describe you. Which of these can be taken away from you? Of course, the answer is that none of them can be taken away by anybody but you. Your "I" is the inner you, your castle, and nobody gets in there unless you let them. So, in the deserted island exercise, the answer is that you are a 10 with or without your roles. Your worth as a person is independent of your role performance.

The problem is that your whole life you have been evaluated based on your roles; you've been conditioned to get your self-esteem from a good role performance. Unfortunately, there's nothing like a year in the sales profession to make you realize you're not as good a role performer as you may have thought you were. One day you make two tough sales and your "R" is a 10; next day you blow an easy close and your "R" is a 2. You make 20 cold calls and everybody blows you off. The rejection factor builds. Then you have a whole month where you can't seem to sell anything to anyone, and you really start to doubt yourself. That's when many salespeople don lifejackets and start looking for the lifeboats.

In the tough times, you should remember that no matter how you perform in your sales role, at the end of the day, your "I" is a 10. The principles, values, and beliefs that make up the inner you have not changed. Learn to separate your role performance from your self-image and also to remain emotionally detached in the selling process. Then you will be better equipped to tackle the difficult daily activities that are required to be successful.

Remember this: The purpose of selling is to go to the bank. You'll achieve that purpose when you:

- Put your ego aside.
- Realize that no matter how your prospects treat you and no matter what results you achieve, your "I" is always a 10.
- Focus your energy on what it takes to close the deal.

Finally, your "I" will always be a 10 and you'll be in sales for the long haul if you remember this basic rule of life: Nobody gets in your castle unless you let them in.

CHAPTER 6

Selling—No Place to Get Your Emotional Needs Met

. . . .

A re you trying to get your emotional needs met in a sales call? On the surface, most salespeople would say, "No." But in reality the truth is quite different. Let's take a look.

Which, if any, of the following common sales problems affect you?

- You want to be liked more than you want to close the sale.
- You're not "assertive enough" (being walked on by prospects).
- Your self-worth is linked to role success.
- You have a fear of rejection.
- You experience call reluctance.
- You have difficulty in dealing with negative prospects.
- You need too much approval from others.
- You are uncomfortable asking for or talking about money.

To one degree or another, all of these issues have to do with your concept of yourself and your need for others to like you, be nice to you, or make you feel OK.

If you want to make it to the top in sales, memorize this rule and say it to yourself every day: "Sales is no place to get my emotional needs met. The purpose of sales is to go to the bank."*

Now let me qualify this for those who are thinking that I'm a cold-hearted mercenary. I love the sales profession, and I enjoy great relationships with my clients. Sales is a rewarding career; I enjoy the thrill of making the sale and then being able to provide a valuable service to my clients. Sales is also fuel for my life. It provides the income I want in order to live the life I want. In summary, I can get my financial and professional needs met in sales—but not my emotional needs.

---

* Source: Sandler Selling System.

Let's explore the *what* and *why* in regards to emotions and sales. If you don't have someplace in your life where you know without a doubt you will receive unconditional love, then you will probably end up looking for love in all the wrong places. For many people, that wrong place is sales. This is not as far-fetched as it sounds. I spoke recently with a salesperson who was treated poorly by a lot of her prospects. They talked down to her, stalled, criticized her prices, never gave definitive answers, and would not tell her where she stood with them. She felt as if she were always in a subservient position to these prospects and had unwittingly bought into the notion that she needed to put up with this in order to make sales. The good news is that she was making a decent living, but she knew she could be more successful and she wanted to feel more comfortable in the sales process.

As we discussed her situation, it came to light that she had grown up with a critical, demanding father. All of her life, he criticized her appearance, her abilities, and her performance. She received no affirmation from the very man who should have provided the unconditional love that every child needs. Result: weak self-concept, lousy self-image, a belief system that told her being abused in a sales call is OK, a high need for somebody to like her, an inability to ask tough questions for fear of upsetting the prospect, and an overall failure to be politely assertive. Bottom line? She was unwittingly trying to get her emotional needs met in her sales calls. All this from a woman who, on the surface, is intelligent, professional, and capable. How much more effective do you think she became once she adjusted her belief systems and had a coat of armor protecting her self-image during a sales call? One thing happened for sure. After a bit of coaching and some introspection, over time this salesperson, through her own program of self-affirmations, began to create "equal business stature" situations for herself, stopped acquiescing to a subservient role, and stopped seeking her emotional well-being in sales calls. Improved sales results followed.

If you ever suffer from any of the sales maladies mentioned earlier, remember these rules to help you stay on task:

- Selling is not for getting your emotional needs met.
- Never become emotionally involved in a sales call.
- No one can enter your castle without your permission.
- When prospects reject you, they're just saying "no" to your product.
- Having a lousy day in sales does not make you a lousy person.
- Don't confuse your self-image with your role as salesperson.

If you want to be all you can be in sales, recognize that, while it is a great profession, it can be a wild ride. Stay off that ride by leaving your emotions in the car during your sales calls. If you do that, you'll enjoy fewer heartaches—and more trips to the bank.

CHAPTER 7

Change or Die

A re you capable of making one single positive change to your selling behavior?

In his 2007 book *Change or Die*, author Alan Deutschman claims that although people have the ability to change their behavior, they rarely do. In fact, the odds are nine-to-one that when faced with a dire need to change, they won't. Most smokers who are presented with a wealth of scientific data on the dangers of tobacco do not quit smoking. Your beliefs are what you feel in your gut, and those beliefs are hard to change; you've spent a lifetime developing and defending them. This explains why providing information rarely changes how people think or act.

This also explains why your best presentation may have absolutely no positive effect on your prospect's desire to buy. Finally, this phenomenon explains why most salespeople keep shoveling information, features, benefits, and fancy presentations at prospects, even though those tactics don't cause people to buy.

Albert Einstein said, "Imagination is more important than knowledge." I believe this is because people see the world through their imagination, not through facts and figures. Deutschman says the same thing in a different way, using terms like ideologies, conceptual frameworks, and belief systems. Whatever you call them, these are the mental structures that shape how people view the world.

Somewhere along the way, early in their sales careers, salespeople can come to view the selling world as a place where they must convince buyers to love the products by providing information, facts, figures, and compelling reasons to buy. Traditional sales training reinforces this notion by emphasizing the presentation as the most important step in the sales process. Somehow people forget that they never bought anything based on a presentation; they buy things because they want or need them, not because a salesperson says they're great.

Would you like to make more sales? Try to make this change to your selling behavior: stop talking about features

and benefits and stop dumping extraneous information, bro-
chures, and fancy PowerPoints on prospects. Wait as long as
you can to tell the prospect anything about your company,
your product, or your service. Spend the first fifteen minutes
talking about the prospect. Find out their problems, concerns, fears, and desires. Make your process about your prospect, not about you.

The problem with that is what we've already said: It's not
easy to change ingrained habits. First of all, it's hard to resist
the temptation to impress your prospects with your knowledge, even though you know, intellectually, that people are
not impressed with knowledge. Secondly, when a prospect
asks a question, you believe that it's your duty to provide an
immediate, detailed answer.

Deutschman's answer to making a difficult behavioral
change is a three-fold process:

- **Relate.** Form a new relationship with a coach or a
  mentor who can inspire you and help you sustain your
  hopes. Support comes in many forms, often from different worlds that can offer different points of view.
- **Repeat.** The new relationship helps you learn, practice, and master the new skills you'll need to be successful. It also helps you create new beliefs about what
  you can accomplish. You're already performing at
  your current belief level; if you want to increase your
  production, you need new beliefs.

- **Reframe.** The new relationship helps you view your problem or situation from a completely different perspective. Example: You no longer try to overcome prospects' objections; you realize that the only person who can do that is the prospect. Therefore you learn a whole new process—reversing—wherein your response to an objection is just a question that will cause the prospect to resolve their own roadblock.

Recognize that while you can change and definitely improve your sales performance, it takes a concerted effort to change long-term, ingrained habits. A half-day get-motivated program won't do it. There are people in your industry making twice as much money as you by selling the same product to the same market as you. There's a reason—behavior. Make a positive change to your selling behavior, and you'll make a positive change to your income.

CHAPTER 8

Three Rules for Sales and Life

D o you have some cardinal rules for ensuring sales success? I asked one of my classes, and here are some they came up with:

- Sell like you are financially independent.
- Listen well, question well.
- You can't sell anybody anything—until they discover they want it.*

---

* Source: Sandler Selling System.

Here are three rules I attempt to apply in my sales efforts. When I apply them successfully, my sales, my business, and my life tend to go well; when I don't—problems.

1. Take responsibility. When you lose a big sale, have a bad month, or don't make quota, is your reaction to look inward for the problem or do you tend to externalize? Externalizing sounds like this:

- "The owner needs to advertise more."
- "The economy is in the pits; nobody's buying now."

These statements may be true to some extent, and that might provide some consolation. The problem is that, valid or not, they won't put food on your table or pay your mortgage. When you take responsibility, you might fix the only thing that you can fix—yourself.

As opposed to externalizing, looking inward for solutions sounds like this:

- "Advertising isn't bringing me the leads I need. I'm going to find my own customers; time to hit the phones and hit the street."
- "Things have changed; with the state of the economy I'm going to need to change my sales activities, be more creative, and stop waiting for business to come to me.

2. Do what you said you would do (even if the only person you told was yourself). Just think of the past week. How many times did somebody tell you they would do something and not do it? "I'll call you with a decision tomorrow," "I'll look at your proposal later today," or "I'll be ready in five minutes." Does it ever frustrate you to hear so many voicemail greetings that say, "Leave me a message, and I'll call you right back," when the reality is that person is unlikely to ever call back?

Now the harder question: How many times last week did you not do something you said you would do? What is that doing to your credibility with clients, prospects—and yourself? Consider the proverb: "Let your 'yes' be 'yes' and your 'no' be 'no.'" Show me a person who always does what they said they would do, and I'll show you a highly respected person.

3. Inspect what you expect. Recently the commanding officer of the *USS George Washington* was dismissed from his command because of a fire onboard his ship. The fire was exacerbated by improper storage of flammable liquids. I sympathize greatly for this man. But the reality is that, while he had a reasonable expectation that the crew would follow the storage procedures, it appears that nobody inspected to make sure. Result—horrible fire, extensive damage, and the end of his Navy career.

Based on expectations and assumptions, what are you hoping is happening in your business? If you expect it, inspect it. Don't just assume something is happening; verify your expectations through observation.

Simple rules for sales, business, and life: Put them on, test them out, and see if things don't go better for you.

CHAPTER 9

It's a Sales World

A while back I attended a one-day intense prospecting training session for salespeople in the heart of downtown London. After nine days of visiting attractions abroad, my wife went off to do the final day by herself so I could endeavor to learn the differences (if any) in the mindset of British salespeople from their American counterparts.

I wondered: Do their prospects act like ours? Do they mislead, gather as much free information as possible, say, "Thanks, that was a great presentation, call me next week," and then enter their version of the witness protection program? Do they say, "We're giving your company top consideration, please submit a proposal," when all they really want is a third quote to support a buying decision they've already made? Do British prospects know fourteen ways to encrypt the phrase, "I need to think it over"? Do they know how to convince a salesperson that they are the one-in-a-million prospect that really will take the call and give an order next week when actually they plan to award that salesperson with a free lifetime subscription to their voicemail? Do they disrespect salespeople's time? Think nothing of missing scheduled appointments? Treat salespeople in ways they would never want to be treated themselves?

Guess what? Prospects are prospects—it matters not what city, continent, or planet they call home. So why do prospects universally engage in this behavior? Because it works. They get all the information and consulting they want without spending a penny. Why does it work? Because salespeople allow it to work.

Yes, really now, you and I are the problem. Salespeople like us allow prospects to treat them this way. Don't believe it? Fill in the blank:

The one constant in every dissatisfying relationship I have ever had, have now, or ever will have is _____.

The correct answer is "me." In every case where a prospect pulled one of the aforementioned shenanigans on you, the one thing that was always present was yourself. Maybe you're the problem. Is that bad news? No, that's good news because the only thing you can fix is yourself. You can't fix prospects. So how do you fix yourself and avoid these problems in the future?

- Remember to take complete responsibility for every sales failure that you experience; don't blame your prospects. After all, you have been a prospect at some time or another, and you've done the same things to salespeople that prospects have done to you.
- Understand that many if not most of your sales problems can be tracked to weak or non-existing verbal agreements between you and your prospects. When a prospect says, "Leave the proposal with me and I'll call you next week," and you comply, that's not an agreement at all. That's smoke. Flush out your prospect's true commitment level with serious questions, your most nurturing tone of voice, and your smoke detector turned on. Don't be afraid to say, "Prospect Person, I get the feeling there's a problem. I'm not comfortable leaving my information with you unless we have a firm commitment on the calendar for our next step."
- Finally, understand that almost all problems you experience in sales are, at their root, conceptual problems. This means that the real problem is a faulty belief system. For example, your prospect says, "Thanks for

the presentation. Let me think it over. I'll call you next week." Your gut tells you, "Nobody ever calls back, and this guy isn't going to either." But your belief system says, "If I tell him that, he's going to think I'm calling him a liar, he'll get mad at me, and then it will be over for sure." So fear takes over. You become compliant and do what he says, and another sale bites the dust. If you want to change the way prospects treat you, change your own belief systems first. This takes time, effort, and possibly some outside coaching or mentoring assistance.

Would you like to stop living on the prospect's system? Do you want to take charge of your sales processes? You can't change prospects; they're the same all over the world. But you sure can change the way you deal with them by first changing yourself. If you do that, you can sell in New York, London, or anywhere else on this planet.

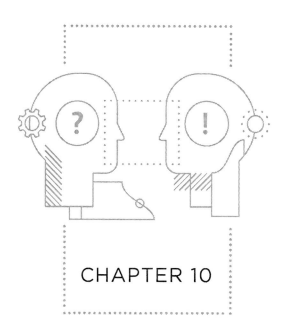

CHAPTER 10

I'm OK, I Think. What about You?

W ere you ever in a sales situation that made you feel not that great? For me, that would cover most of my first two years in sales. Thank goodness I closed enough deals to keep going, but I wondered, "Why do these prospects always seem to get the best of me? Why am I on top of the world one week and totally defeated the next? When will I get off this emotional roller-coaster?"

Finally Coach Jim, my sales mentor, taught me the most

important concept to master to thrive in sales: You've got to be OK being not-OK.

Early in life, people rely on their parents to do things for them that they could not do for themselves. Each person comes to the realization that they are small and the world is big. To one degree or another, everyone feels a sense of powerlessness in the face of a vast universe.

These things can make you feel not-OK. Most people retain some of those not-OK feelings as they grow. If you had nurturing parents, you received a lot of OK messages, too. Hopefully they were enough to overcome the not-OK messages. If not, then you might have used the tried-and-true childhood coping mechanism of appeasement: "Maybe if I give Dad what he wants he'll be nice to me." My dad's approval was so important to me that I used to prop my math test results on his dresser so he'd see them.

The process of growing forms the four basic life positions of OK-ness (from the bestseller *I'm OK—You're OK* by Thomas Harris):

1. **I'm not-OK; you're OK.** This is the most common, although not very healthy, life position. Many people move into not-OK feelings on a regular basis. Meeting new people is generally a source of feeling not-OK, which is why prospecting in sales is so difficult. People with a high need for approval are usually looking to connect with some type of authority figure—parent,

boss, or client—in order to elicit "strokes" or verbal recognition. Since prospecting usually provides more negative than positive strokes, prospecting is viewed as an emotionally risky (not-OK) venture, and salespeople become experts at avoiding it.

2. **I'm not-OK; you're not-OK.** This is not a normal or healthy life position. When children grow up with a severe absence of nurturing, they feel they are not-OK. As they mature, they begin to believe that everyone is not-OK. In turn, they do not trust people who give them strokes, either positive or negative.

3. **I'm OK; you're not-OK.** This is another undesirable life position. Some children who grow up with critical or abusive parents somehow convince themselves that they are the only OK thing in an entirely not-OK world. They externalize all problems, sales or otherwise, rarely taking responsibility for improving their own performance. People with this life position rarely make effective salespeople.

4. **I'm OK; you're OK.** This, of course, is a healthy life position, one that most adults consciously attempt to achieve. When you operate out of this position, you tend to deal better with the ups and downs of sales; you don't take it personally when a prospect says, "Get lost."

So what did Coach Jim mean when he told me, "You've got to be OK being not-OK"? I think he meant a few things:

1. You're not going to get your emotional needs met in sales (see Chapter 6). The profession is for making money.
2. The best way to be successful in sales is to fail early, fail often, and fail fast—and get used to it. (See Chapter 4.)
3. In sales, you'll end up in a lot of potentially humiliating situations. If you can't handle that, find another line of work.
4. Prospects and clients don't control how you feel; you do.

OK/not-OK is the WD-40 of life. If you master the principle of feeling OK about yourself, especially in situations like prospecting, asking for money, and being assertive, you'll be able to do the difficult things needed to be a successful salesperson.

CHAPTER 11

Oh, the Humility!
Are You OK
Being Not-OK?

I n the Navy, I was a tough guy: captain of an attack submarine, the nemesis of many Soviet skippers, ready to go toe-
to-toe with any enemy, and willing to face death on a daily
basis. If the bad guys weren't enough, every second of every
day, Mother Ocean was trying to get in my submarine and
swallow me whole. No problem! Bring it on, Mother! Davy
Jones' locker (that age-old sailors' euphemism for drowning)

did not scare me. I was truly in my element at sea, and I was definitely OK.

How quickly all of that changed when I came into sales and tried to make my first cold call. Suddenly I was not-OK. My hands were shaking, my voice was quivering, I stumbled and stuttered through my script, and I was so relieved when the lady I called said, "No thanks!" and hung up.

The irony of being terrified by a phone call set me on a path to discover the source of my fear and anxiety. Here's what I figured out.

The prestige associated with my role as a submarine officer always helped me feel very OK about myself. I was respected, revered, and obeyed. In case of doubt, I sported my sheriff's badge that read "Commanding Officer," i.e. "Big Shot."

In sales, trying to get leads, trying harder to get leads to return my calls, fighting to keep customers who were being wooed by competitors, prospects taking my valuable proposals and entering that witness protection program, hearing "no" on a daily basis—all made me very not-OK. I was not respected, revered, or obeyed; I wasn't the captain, and I wasn't a big shot.

So, at the ripe old age of 40-plus, I had to dig down deep and find something to like about myself beyond my titles and status in the world. I had to learn to be OK being not-OK.

If you ever find the frustrations, humiliation, and embarrassment of sales seem to outweigh the successes, consider these points:

- Selling is a Broadway play put on by a psychiatrist. Buying is and should be an emotional experience for the prospect, not the seller. If you become emotionally involved in the outcome of a sales call, it will be hard to close. Keep your composure and objectivity as a psychiatrist does.
- Always let your buyer preserve their dignity. You don't have to let people abuse you, but it is also not smart to focus on your own feelings. Help others feel OK about themselves.
- Stop trying to look so professional; try struggling a bit. One way to get people to be comfortable around you is to not have all the answers—don't be too polished, too know-it-all. Learn to struggle naturally, and prospects will want to bail you out. Be not-OK on purpose.

It took a long time, but I finally arrived in a place where prospects and selling no longer control how I feel about myself. I'm OK without my sheriff's badge, and I'm OK being not-OK.

How about you? Are you OK in the world of sales? You are a winner because of what is inside you, not what's happening on the outside. Remember that and you will always be OK being not-OK.

CHAPTER 12

Who Said It?

A s a group, salespeople are some of the most not-OK people in society. That's a broad indictment, but as a salesperson myself I know it can be true. During my career in the Navy, people tended to respect me because of the insignia on my collar. Coming out of that environment into the sales world, everything was different; no more R-E-S-P-E-C-T just for showing up. Cold calls were difficult, even demeaning; asking for money was embarrassing; hearing "no" was painful.

So many nights, on the way home, there was a little voice

inside me saying, "Too tough, too tough; maybe I should just give up this sales thing and get a nice safe desk job." What scared little boy said that? Survival in sales meant finding a way to feel good about myself as a person no matter what happened in my sales call. For that reason, I turned to transactional analysis (TA).

TA is a human relations model that is useful in understanding and improving your interactions with prospects. In this model, the personality is segmented into three ego states; each can be thought of as an audio tape that records and plays back at various times in life:

- **Parent ego state:** From birth to about age six, the Parent tape recorded all the messages that came in, principally from authority figures: parents, older siblings, pre-school teachers. These are the how-to's in life, the shoulds and shouldn'ts, the permissions and non-permissions. Early in life, children tend to accept this information without question. The Parent state can be 1) Critical ("Can't you do anything right?") or 2) Nurturing ("I know you can do it!").

- **Child ego state:** The Child tape records simultaneously with the Parent tape, but instead of recording the incoming messages, it records emotional responses. The Child ego state is the feelings part of your personality. If you are sad, mad, glad, or scared, or if you are using words such as "I," "me," "mine," "I want," "I wish," "I hope," then you are in your Child ego state. The most debilitating malady in all of sales, the need to be liked, comes from the Child state and affects salespeople more than they will admit or even realize.

- **Adult ego state:** The Adult tape starts recording at about age ten months and keeps recording for the rest of your life. Do you remember Mr. Spock in the original TV show *Star Trek*? He was always in the Adult state—rational, logical, analytical, and unemotional. The Adult state is your command central because it is the one, when well-developed, that appropriately turns the other states on and off. One of the goals of TA is to help you develop your Adult to better command your other ego states.

The most effective communications take place when people operate out of their Adult state. Unfortunately, many sales situations cause people to abandon their Adult state and take on a Critical Parent or Child approach to selling. The biggest obstacle to developing sales success is typically the Parent tape. The Parent tape shackles you to messages from your past. For example:

- Fear of cold calls can be linked to a parent's admonition, "Don't talk to strangers," or "Don't bother people."
- Fear of discussing money or asking for the check at the close is usually linked to a parent telling you, "It's not nice to talk about money."

- You may even have heard a parent exclaim, "That person ripped me off—salespeople are crooks!" This could cause you to feel less than OK about being in sales.

The next obstacle is the Child tape. Your Child most likely learned early on to externalize painful situations, and it shows up in sales:

- "He wouldn't buy from anyone!"
- "Nobody can sell at these prices!"
- "I wonder if she likes me. She didn't seem happy with my price."

As long as salespeople externalize their selling problems, those problems will persist. The Child avoids taking responsibility for its behavior when doing so would be too painful. What to do? Obviously your Child and Parent tapes can sabotage your best sales intentions. The solution is to:

1. Develop your Adult as the executive of your personality.
2. Leave your Child in the car during sales calls.
3. Be a Nurturing Parent with prospects and with yourself, but leave your Critical Parent at home.

When I started doing those things I stopped feeling not-OK, stopped giving voice to the scared little boy within, and started getting mentally tough. Sales success soon followed as did a renewed sense of confidence and self-worth.

CHAPTER 13

Stay Adult and Leave Your Child Behind

"When a man is wrapped up in himself,
he makes a rather small package."

—JOHN RUSKIN

Most salespeople, at one time or another, get emotionally involved in a sales call. This mistake is one of the major mental roadblocks in the sales profession.

Who can blame you? You fight for leads, make the

prospecting calls, scrape up a few appointments and then finally get a meeting with a potential buyer—no wonder you can get excited at the wrong time.

When a buyer says, "I really like what I see; you're about to make a big sale," it's tough not to get "happy ears" on and start calculating the commission.

But that's when you're giving away your valuable information or proposal, with no real assurance as to what's going to happen next, only to have that formerly enthusiastic prospect disappear, along with the proposal. Imagine if you always thought and reacted in the sales process with the calculated approach of a seasoned brain surgeon, systematically working through the procedure, reading and reacting to the situation and focusing on fixing the patient's problem—no "happy ears" there, just lots of closed sales.

As described in Chapter 12, the Child ego state is that part of your personality that gets emotional. If you're sad, glad, mad, or scared—typical reactions in a sales call—you're in your Child ego state. That's a useful part of your personality. Without it, humans would all be rather dull people. But during a sales call, learn to leave your Child behind. Learn to stay an Adult—logical, analytical, and intensely aware of your prospect's words, gestures, emotions, and unspoken messages. Imagine during your sales call that you are a third party, looking at the engaged salesperson (you) and your buyer from a fly-on-the-wall perspective. Here are some ways to stay third party and keep your emotions in check when meeting with buyers.

1. Recognize that buyers are human and prone to being defensive when meeting with a salesperson. The best salespeople are amateur psychologists. They understand that everything a buyer does is a reflection of scripts they carry in their head. Don't get upset by things buyers say or do to you.

2. Check your own psychological maturity. Do you spend more time acting like a parent (smothering, controlling, and criticizing), a child (complaining and whining), or an adult (composed and confident)? The more time you spend in the Adult ego state, the more you can observe what is happening in your sales meetings from an objective viewpoint.

3. Probe with meaningful questions. This causes the buyer to do most of the talking and allows you to listen, think, and reflect during the answers.

4. Listen with your eyes and inner ear. Buyers will not always tell you directly how they feel about you and your company. But they will give you lots of information with their tonality, body language, and hidden messages. For example: "You've given me a lot to think about. Leave this bid and call me next week." Translation: "I need this information to do some price shopping."

5. If attacked, respond from your Adult head, not your Child's gut. If a buyer is sarcastic, aggressive, or cynical, don't respond in kind. Remember, there's no "up yours" in sales. Just take a deep breath, and ask, "Prospect Person, can you tell me what happened to make you feel this way?"

6. Get into the buyer's shoes. A little empathy might go a long way. If you were the prospect and had to deal with a salesperson like you, how would you feel?

7. Focus on the buyer and the sale, not on protecting your ego. Listen to your inner voice of reason and objectivity—your "personal sales coach." Always respond non-defensively.

Professional quarterbacks have an earpiece in their helmets. Their coaches methodically call in the plays to them as the team huddles. Reacting emotionally to the success or failure of the last play will not serve the coach or quarterback well. They stay adults. The good news is that you can, too. There's no need to get emotional during your sales calls; just leave your Child behind.

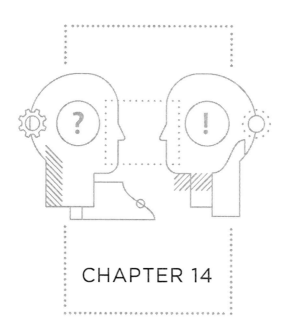

CHAPTER 14

Aim to Speak to Your Client's Inner Child

P eople at my age and older spend a lot of time nursing and favoring sore joints—shoulders, hips, knees, and ankles. In general, most physical therapists and orthopedic specialists tend to treat each of these joint problems as an isolated situation. Anatomical functionalist and author Pete Egoscue says that the eight major load-bearing joints in our bodies are all connected. When one is out of alignment, it can affect things in other locations.

It's so easy in sales to think that the problem is closing

the deal. Many salespeople think that if they had a better set of closing lines, they would make more sales. In essence, they treat their lack of sales success as an isolated problem—a weak close—when the real problem is something else. If you're getting in front of enough prospects but not closing the deals, it's likely a symptom of not discovering "pain," or the true motive for buying, rather than a weak closing step.

As was said earlier, TA defines three ego states that influence our behavior—the Parent, the Adult, and the Child. The Parent ego state stores information about what is right or wrong, good or bad, acceptable or unacceptable. The Adult ego state is the logical, rational part of your makeup. It weighs the pros and cons of a situation without the emotional involvement. The Child is the emotional part of your makeup; this is where feelings and emotions are stored—feelings and emotions that influence you your entire life, whether you are buying, selling, or doing something else entirely. The Child is where most decisions originate. The Child is the little six-year-old within, who, when feeling a particular emotion says, "I want that."

In sales, it is important to realize that the prospect's Child ego starts the selling process. The Parent will not judge whether a purchase is right, and the Adult will not weigh in on the pros and cons of a product unless there is an emotion driving the process. In other words. the Parent and the Adult will not get involved until the Child says, "I want it!"

Getting your prospect's Child to express that desire is the

objective of discovering pain in selling. Discovering pain does not necessarily mean your prospect will act outwardly emotional, but it does mean that inside their Child is saying, "I want it." A good outward indicator of a prospect in pain is hearing something like, "I'm so frustrated with my current situation." Unfortunately most salespeople never hear those words because they are too busy presenting features of their products to listen for their prospect's pain. Once they have made their presentation, they jump to the close and then wonder why the prospect said, "Looks great. I need some time to think it over." Prospects in pain don't think it over; they make decisions.

What will make your prospect's Child say, "I want it"? It might be because you helped them see things from a different perspective. Perhaps your questions helped them self-discover something they didn't know before; maybe your discussion uncovered some doubt about a current strategy. Whatever the motivation, you're less likely to close a sale unless your prospect's inner Child gets emotionally involved first. Omitting this step or doing a superficial job will result in a lukewarm prospect on your hands, one who sees you and your product as a commodity that can be gotten somewhere else, and probably at a better price.

CHAPTER 15

Emotional Buying—You Can't Sell without It

People buy emotionally—everyone has heard that. But what does it really mean? It means that while people make buying decisions emotionally, they justify these decisions intellectually. To further understand this concept, it helps to know who is making the decisions and who is justifying the decisions.

Remember (see Chapter 12), TA tells us that there are three ego states within each of us: Parent, Adult, and Child. In his bestseller *I'm OK—You're OK*, author Thomas Harris writes that it is as if within each person there is "the same little person" they were when they were three years old. There are also within them their own parents. These are "recordings in the brain of actual internal and external events," the most significant of which happened in the first five years of their life.

For better or worse, that Parent is always with you, telling you what you should and should not do. Your Child is the emotional being within you; whenever you are mad, sad, glad, or scared, you are in your Child ego state. Lastly, the Adult is the logical, rational, decision-making, information-seeking part of your makeup, never emotional, always carefully weighing the pros and cons of any situation.

In order for your prospect to decide to buy from you, the Child in them has to get emotionally involved in the process. The Child has to think, "I really want this, I need it, and it will help solve my problem." This is why in your sales process, you should ask questions that will evoke from your prospect their pain. Once you have found the problems, you should continue probing to find the underlying reasons, the effect on your prospect, previous efforts to correct the situation, and the personal impact on them of continuing to live with the situation. A well-crafted questioning strategy will evoke a prospect's inner Child and an emotional decision to buy, assuming that your product is an appropriate solution to the problem.

So far, so good. But if you rush to close too quickly, you risk sabotaging the sale or evoking buyer's remorse later on.

That's because the Critical Parent and the Adult have not been properly involved in the process and the Child will lose interest rather quickly. Then the Parent will step in and say, "Can't you live without this? You don't have extra money to spend right now." Meanwhile the Adult asks, "Does this make sense for you? Is this the best use of your resources?" In this case, the Child may have made an emotional decision to buy, but the decision was not justified intellectually. Now your sale is in jeopardy.

In order to involve everybody, make sure that after you diagnose your prospect's problem, you pin down their ability and willingness to pay for your solution. As you question them on their budget, their Adult can get involved and see if the expense makes sense. Then you should determine their decision-making process so you'll know what it will take to get a decision. Proper questioning here will get the Parent involved in stating what it would take in the way of a presentation to move forward with the sale.

Once everybody (Parent, Adult, and Child) is on board and properly involved, you can move to the presentation of your product or service. This is where you show your prospect how you will solve their pain. Since you've already addressed the buying motive, budget, and decision-making processes, you've cleared out the three biggest across-the-board objections in sales: suitability of product or service; price; and ability to make a decision. Therefore your presentation should result in a *yes/no* decision from your prospect—not a "We'll think it over," "Your price is too high," or "Call us in two weeks after the boss reviews it." Most importantly, a buying decision should be firm and not subject to buyer's remorse.

Learn to appeal to all three ego states within your prospect; help them justify the emotional need to buy. Then you will see buying decisions made more quickly, and you will also see your buyers remaining committed to the decisions they make.

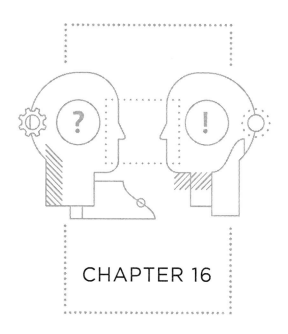

CHAPTER 16

No-Brainer Decisions

How do your prospects make buying decisions? Too slowly for your liking? Perhaps there's been a time when you wanted to say, "Prospect Person, I can see you're having a tough time with this decision, but frankly, it's the biggest no-brainer in the history of Earth!"

There's a mortgage guy on my local radio who has great commercials. He's disarmingly honest, saying things like:

- "Make no mistake, I'm running this commercial to make money."
- "I'm not your father."

- "I charge no fees or closing costs, but I still make plenty of money."

That gives me a good feeling. I figure if he is willing to be honest about those things, he'll probably be truthful with me if we do business together. He has another expression I like, too: "It's the biggest no-brainer in the history of Earth," as if it should be a piece of cake to make the decision to buy from him. But there's a problem with that—it ignores the fact that everybody has their own decision-making process. The frustrations, fears, and hesitations that you experience in making buying decisions are exactly what your prospects are going through. A no-brainer for one person is a gut-wrenching decision for another. Let's take a look at how most people make decisions.

Everybody has an internal "board of directors" that guides their decision-making process. I've heard it described as six distinct voices; each person gives different weight to these voices as they make decisions.

- **Inner self.** "I'll help you understand how your own personal dreams and desires impact the decision." This is the visionary in you, thinking about your hopes and dreams for the future. Some people spend a lot of time dreaming. If you tap into your prospect's dreams, you may sway this board member to your side.
- **Judgmental thinking.** "I'll help you understand how your 'shoulds' about others affect your decision." Your

judgments about how other people should behave or live their lives may impact your thinking, especially when your decisions affect others.

- **Self-concept.** "I'll help you understand how your 'shoulds' about yourself affect your decision." Your concept of yourself, whether you should take risks or whether you deserve something, will impact your choices. For example, no matter how much I want something new, there's always a voice in the back of my head, saying, "If what you have is not totally worn out and used up, buying a new one is a waste of money and you should not do it." (Remember that your prospect may experience guilt about spending a lot of money on themself.)

- **Outer self.** "I'll help you understand how your decision will affect how others perceive you." After ten years of driving my old, beat-up pickup truck on sales calls (the same one I take to the dump on weekends), a friend of mine casually commented that it wasn't doing much for my image. He advised that there were people who actually would hesitate to do business with me if they saw what I was driving. He reminded me of a simple point I had apparently ignored—image matters. But my self-concept ("You don't deserve a new car") was in conflict with my outer self ("Prospects will perceive you as unsuccessful because you drive a hunk of junk"). After three more months of combat, outer self won and I bought a new car.

- **Intuition/empathy.** "I'll help you understand how this decision will emotionally affect others." People who are high on empathy will care greatly about the impact their decisions and purchases have on others. For example, I care a lot more about a reliable car for my wife than for myself so I'd rather buy her a new car.
- **Practical thinking.** "I'll help you understand how the decision will work out in practical, common sense terms." This board member is your resident Adult: analytical, unemotional, and fact-oriented and wants to be right more than anything else.

Nobody gives equal weighting to the six votes provided by this decision-making panel. Use your questioning skills (see Chapter 15) to uncover which of these factors will have the most weight in your prospect's decision making. If you help your prospects feel more comfortable with their decisions, you'll be more likely to get decisions. That's the no-brainer that will take you to the bank.

CHAPTER 17

No Room for Games

D o your prospects play games and engage in power plays with you? Power plays put people in situations where everybody loses; they are techniques used to get people to do things they do not want to do. A power play is an effort by a prospect to put a salesperson in an inferior position and eliminate any chance of a level playing field between the two. Power plays usually deteriorate into games. Your job is to avoid or neutralize the effects of power plays and games in the sales situation.

A good sales relationship is based on the assumption that

both the prospect and the seller have an interest in doing things for each other. Part of gutsy selling is to believe that you as a salesperson have rights and that you and your prospect need to deal with each other on an Adult-to-Adult basis. When a prospect starts to play games with you, you need to gently "call the game" in order to keep things on an Adult level. Games are insincere transactions between people. According to the Karpman Drama Triangle, there are three possible positions in a game. All three positions tend to externalize, meaning they avoid responsibility for their situation and never discuss the real problem.

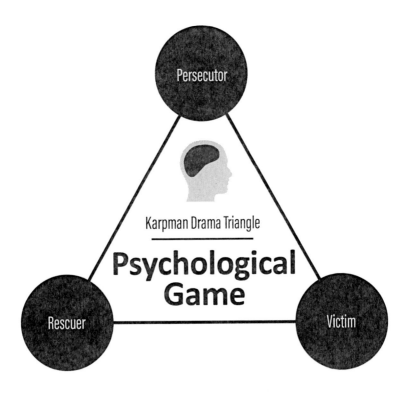

The Drama Triangle includes:

1. A **persecutor**, who does something hurtful to someone else in the power play without permission, such as create guilt, discomfort, or pain.
2. A **victim**, who receives the persecutor's action and tends to look for a victimized role. Their games include: "pity poor me," "isn't it awful," and others. The victim always has excuses and never accepts responsibility for their own behavior.
3. A **rescuer**, who looks for someone to rescue without being asked.

The rules of the game are that everybody keeps moving around the triangle, constantly changing roles.

One of my clients owns a landscaping business. She had a client who signed up for a significant overhaul of his yard. She told him she expected to have the job done in two weeks. Weather problems interfered, and she was unable to complete the job on schedule. At this point, the customer accused her of making empty promises ("now I've got you"), claimed she had spoiled his plans ("pity poor me"), and demanded a refund. He started out as persecutor, shifted to victim, and was making a play to get her to rescue him. When my client did not immediately acquiesce with a refund, he shifted back to persecutor, commenced name calling, and threatened legal action.

The best thing to do when a customer starts playing games is to call the game.

1. Don't get emotionally involved. If you call the game harshly and blow up, the prospect becomes the victim (a role they may like). They'll eventually turn into the persecutor and punish you by not buying from you. If you call the game gently and with a sense of humor, you can level the playing field.
2. Stop the game as soon as possible and stay out once it is over. A simple phrase like, "I get the feeling you're upset," or, "Hmmm, sounds like there's absolutely nothing I could do to regain your trust," will normally stop the game.
3. Use a specific verbal agreement to establish and maintain a straight Adult-to-Adult relationship.

In the situation above, the landscaper said to the irate customer, "I'm sorry for the delays. This has certainly been frustrating for all of us. At this point we can focus on placing blame for something neither you nor I can control—the weather—or we can discuss how to move ahead and get this project done. How should we proceed?"

Games begin when people discount the real problem or the significance of the problem. Salespeople discount the real problem every time they say, "All prospects are liars." That may or may not be true, but the real problem is using that as an excuse for poor sales or failing to learn how to deal appropriately with people who are lying.

In this case, the salesperson is the (self-made) victim; the liars (all prospects) are the persecutors; and the rescuer may be any sympathetic ear who says, "You're right—they never tell the truth. It's a wonder that anybody can sell anything!" The problem with discounting and failing to recognize the real issues here is that this salesperson is inflicting unnecessary pain on themself.

An appropriate response from a sales manager in the above situation might be, "Anna, you're right. Prospects don't always tell us the truth. But complaining about it won't help us build our business. Let's figure out what you're doing that causes prospects to want to mislead you, and then let's fix it." This "calls the game" and puts Anna on notice that she can't fix prospects; she can only fix herself.

When you find yourself in the middle of a game, either with prospects or other salespeople, call the game, both gently and in a nurturing way. Be politely assertive as you bring the conversation and relationship back to an Adult-to-Adult basis and level the playing field.

CHAPTER 18

How to Avoid the Games People Play

For professionally trained salespeople, work is fun—most of the time. But once in a while a prospect or even a client can say or do something that gets under your skin. When that happens, you can:

- Enter your Child ego state, respond from your inner victim, and feel hurt, angry, or abused.
- Enter your Parent ego state and become a persecutor or a rescuer.

- Stay Adult and realize they're trying to draw you into a psychological game.

Recently George, a business owner, visited me to discuss training for his company. I invited him to sit down. He replied, "I don't need to sit, I only need you to tell me two things: What makes you think you are so good that you can help my people, and how much is this going to cost?"

I took a deep breath to allow for time to think and realized I was being invited into a game.

Some reasons people play games are to elicit psychological strokes (verbal positive and negative messages), to justify their own life position (e.g., "I'm not-OK, you're OK"), or to get something they want but are afraid to ask for. You might have played games like this at some point in your life. However, games hinder communication by enabling the players to avoid the real issues and directing their energy towards the game rather than resolving those issues.

The best way to deal with a game you have been drawn into is to stop playing. Revert to your Adult ego state when you think a prospect is drawing you in. Don't rescue the prospect, don't go on the attack and persecute, and don't take on a victim role. In the case mentioned above, I knew that there were two very tempting responses that would get me nowhere: fight or flight.

- **Fight:** "George, I don't like the way this meeting is

starting; unless you sit down and answer my questions I don't think I'll be able to answer yours!"

- **Flight:** "Sure thing, George. Here is a list of testimonials, a price sheet, and my card; take the info, think it over, and call me if you have any further interest."

I've botched enough sales calls in the past to know not to do those things anymore. Since I can't use either of these responses, I ask myself what would my Adult do? My Adult wants to move beyond the emotions to sorting things out logically and figuring out the best course of action.

Here's how the conversation proceeded with George.

Me: I'm uneasy that I may not be able to help you or your people at all.

George: Why would you say that?

Me: I get the feeling you're more worried that I might sell you something than you are interested in us working together to figure out a possible way to help your team.

George: Well, I still need you to answer those questions!

Me: Perhaps you would let me ask you a few questions first? At this point I don't know if I can help your folks at all. What they're doing now may already be better than what I can teach them, and I won't know the cost until we map out a solution together. How should we proceed?

George: All right, let's talk.

The goal is to get the prospect into an Adult-to-Adult conversation. Unless your prospect sees you as a peer and not somebody to boss around, it is likely that you will be selling on their terms at best, or worse, providing a lot of unpaid consulting.

Stay out of games with these tips:

1. Learn to recognize a game as it is forming. Understand what ego state people are coming from and don't let them hook your Parent or Child state.
2. Take ownership of your feelings and vulnerabilities in front of others. Don't be afraid to tell prospects (or others) if you don't think a conversation is going well for both parties.
3. Stay Adult. In transactional analysis, this is known as "calling the game."

Games like chess, Monopoly, and canasta produce real winners and real losers. Psychological games produce only losers, both in sales and in life. If your buyer says something that makes you feel uncomfortable, it's possible that the game is starting. Call the game early; everyone will come out a winner in the end.

CHAPTER 19

Childhood Messages, Life Scripts, and Sales Success

Your mother probably told you, "Never talk to strangers." Good rule or bad rule? It's a great rule for your seven-year-old daughter, but it's a lousy rule for a twenty-seven-year-old salesperson. For better or worse, we all have life scripts programmed into our beings and it is difficult to overcome them. In her landmark book *Born to Win*, Dr. Muriel James writes: "Children are not born with their feelings already programmed towards objects and people. Each child learns toward whom to show affection, whom to fear, whom to hate, and about what to feel guilty." She also quotes Dr. Eric Berne, the founder of transactional analysis, who said that people are born free, but one of the first things they learn is to do as they are told. They then spend the rest of their life doing that. Thus the "first enslavement" is to the parents. People follow their instructions "forevermore," retaining only in some cases the right to choose their own methods and consoling themselves "with an illusion of autonomy."

Wow, that's heavy stuff. Imagine the idea that you and I, grown adults, are still doing just what our parents taught us, no more, no less. For the most part, that's probably a good thing, assuming your parents taught you good stuff. But when it comes to sales, many of those good parental rules may not be serving you too well, and you are probably more beholden to them than you think.

For example, when I was in the ninth grade, my mother found out that I was asking other boys in the lunchroom for spare change to buy ice-cream sandwiches. She got me by the collar and looked me square in the eye, saying, "Don't ever let me hear of you asking other boys for lunch money; if you need lunch money you come to me. People in our family don't ask others for money!" Guess which part of that message has always stuck with me? When I came into the sales world, it took me a year and the help of my sales coach to figure out that I was afraid to ask people for money. I failed to tell people at the end of our first meeting that they would need to make a down payment at the next meeting and therefore they should bring their checkbook with them. Result: a lot of delays, more think-it-overs, longer sales cycles, and more objections.

When good old Coach Jim found out about this money problem, he put me on a program of daily affirmations (positive self-talk and motivational/belief statements) about the importance of discussing money up front with my prospects. I still have those statements (my original sales affirmations) in my sales journal. Here's one: "It's OK, in fact it's a good thing, to ask people for money. When they pay me, I am helping them create a plan for long-term success. It's a win-win for everybody. Don't be afraid to ask people for money—they can always say, 'no.'"

What childhood messages do you have standing between you and sales success? Not everybody has money hang-ups, but most salespeople have some sort of self-limiting concept that stifles sales success. Here are some messages that may be scripted into you from early in life:

- "Money doesn't grow on trees."
- "Don't be too successful, honey; it might scare people away."
- "It's not nice to bother people."
- "Our family has always made it on our own; we'd rather starve than ask for help."

- "Be seen and not heard."
- "Don't interrupt."

Can you imagine how each of these might limit a salesperson? If you believe it's not nice to bother people, how will you ever feel OK about prospecting, knocking on doors, making cold calls, or starting a conversation with a stranger in an elevator? If you're afraid of success—and many people are—you'll always be satisfied with sales mediocrity, making just enough to get by and being comfortable with the status quo. (Remember: Comfortable equals poor.)

If you are experiencing limited sales success, take a look at your childhood messages and life scripts. They have their place and purpose. But your parents probably did not know you were going to grow up to be a salesperson. If they had known, they might have said, "Sweetie, we love you and want you to be careful, but you need to get out and talk to twenty strangers every day. And don't forget to ask them for money!"

CHAPTER 20

Take Out the Head Trash

H ave you ever attended a one-day sales seminar—
packed with great closing tactics, nifty ideas for
overcoming objections, and slick methods for deliv-
ering rock 'em, sock 'em presentations—only to find yourself
a few days later doing the same things you did before the
seminar? What happened? Where did all the great ideas go?
Why didn't you implement what you learned?

When I was 16, my father paid for me to take some golf
lessons from a local pro. After several sessions, the pro told

me it was time to get on the links and play a round on my own. I set up on the first tee and got ready to swing when four old men (well, old to me, anyway) came up behind me waiting their turn. Their staring made me a nervous wreck. After three lousy shots, I still was not far enough along the fairway for them to tee off. It seemed like the whole world was watching me flail. Not wanting to further embarrass myself, I picked up my ball and went home and haven't tried golf since.

The pro taught me a lot of useful skills and tactics—grips, swings, stances, and the like. But he never touched on the fears, anxieties, and doubts that lay between my ears. I didn't have the conceptual tools needed to deal with embarrassment and humiliation—real or imagined.

Short-term sales training typically addresses sales skills. Attendees learn great tactics from masterful sales trainers. But this same training never covers the conceptual problems—head trash—that plague most sales or business development professionals. All the skill training in the world won't help much if the head trash is not eliminated first.

Here are five conceptual problems that affect, at one time or another and to one degree or another, almost everyone in sales.

1. **Buy cycle.** How do you treat salespeople? Do you bust their chops for a lower price, pump them for free information, and then say you need to "think it over"?

People sell the way they buy and buy the way they sell. However you treat salespeople is how you will expect and allow prospects to treat you. If you can't make a decision, don't expect your prospects to either. If you want to stop getting think-it-overs, make this pledge now: "I will never again tell a salesperson I need to think it over. It's 'yes' or 'no' for me—nothing else."

2. **Need for approval:** Most human beings want to be liked. It's more fun than being not liked. But a problem begins when you want to be liked more than you want to make a sale. Everyone has psychological trash they're carrying around. A lot of it has to do with not being liked or loved by the right people—parents, spouses, and friends. So you take these unmet needs into sales calls. If you want to leave a sales call with your prospect liking you more than you want to leave with their check, you might have an approval problem. Remember—sales is no place to get your emotional needs met; sales is the place to go to the bank.

3. **Negative scripts:** When I was in third grade, our neighbors bought a new car. As my parents and I marveled at it, I asked, "How much did it cost?" Mom reminded me that it's not nice to ask about money. Years later I came into sales and had to ask prospects about money on a daily basis. But Mom was standing on my shoulder telling me that's not nice. Everyone has scripts from early in life floating around their heads:

"Don't talk to strangers"; "Don't bother people"; "You'll never amount to much"; "It's never OK to fail"; and others. Examine your scripts and make sure they are not standing in the way of your sales success.

4. **Becoming emotionally involved:** When your mortgage payment depends on making a sale or when you think you're about to finally close the big one, it's tough to stay objective. Think about an explosives specialist. You don't want them getting nervous or excited when they're defusing a bomb. Whether it's reality or not, your attitude in front of a prospect should always be: "I'd love to work with you, but I'm financially independent and I don't need your business." Once you are emotionally involved in a sales process, you'll find it difficult to be objective and you won't be able to negotiate from a position of strength.

5. **Money concept:** How much do you really believe you are worth? How much do you really believe your services are worth? If you grew up without a whole lot of money, it's likely that deep down you have a belief that you're not really worth very much. In sales you can work for days or weeks without making anything, and then one day in about an hour you can make a $9,000 commission; that is, if you can bear the intense negotiating skills of your prospect who's threatening to cancel the sale if you don't lower the price. But if you have a weak money concept, you might start to

waver, feel guilty, and lower the price—and your commission—in the process. Remember, you are making exactly what you believe you are worth, not a penny more or less. Start believing you are worth more and you might start making more.

Conceptual problems are not easily or quickly corrected. Doing so takes a concerted, long-term effort. Typically, this involves gaining:

- A new relationship with a coach, support group, accountability partner or teammate. In this relationship, you can explore and seek help on conceptual issues that are holding you back.
- A new habit or tactic to overcome the problem, such as a way to comfortably discuss money or a new, more determined approach to making your own buying decisions. Over time, with the help of your coach, you repeat this new behavior and make it second nature.
- A new, positive, belief system in which you reframe your former, negative, beliefs to support the new, healthier habits. For example: "It's a good thing for me, when I'm the buyer, to only tell salespeople 'yes' or 'no.' When I'm more decisive, so are my prospects."

If you want to hit a hole-in-one in sales, take the head trash out first. Then, you'll have the emotional ability to put your great skills to work.

CHAPTER 21

There Are No Bad Prospects, Just Bad Salespeople

Are you mentally and emotionally tough enough to handle the world of sales?

Most sales professionals, when asked that, will answer that mental and emotional toughness is one of their strengths. To accurately gauge yourself in this area, consider this question: What upsets you as you go about your activities in the world of sales? In a matter of seconds, you can probably come up with five to ten things that upset you. Take a minute and make a list.

"I get upset when prospects..."

- ...tell me that they want to think it over."
- ...can't seem to make a decision."
- ...use my proposals to price shop all over town."
- ...don't seem to know what the appointment is about."
- ...don't show up for appointments."

These things are indeed frustrating to salespeople. But the real problem is salespeople defining their problems in terms of their prospects' behavior. Business owners frequently tell me, "You don't understand—we're dealing with a tough market. Our prospects have lots of choices." This point of view avoids taking responsibility for your own failure or success. If you blame your problems on your prospects, how will you ever be able to fix the problems? You can't fix what you can't control, and you can't control prospects. Complaining about the way prospects act or treat you makes as much sense as a sailor complaining about rough seas.

Prospects will do what prospects do—mislead, delay, stall, be deliberately noncommittal, act indecisively, take your free information—and they're not going to change for you. It's important to remember that they have been programmed by traditional salespeople to be on their guard against being "sold," lied to, or tricked. Accordingly, all prospects have survival techniques, which they are ready to use whenever a salesperson walks through the door. That doesn't mean that prospects are bad people; they are just defending themselves against a perceived enemy. It's up to you to take control of the selling situation—to make prospects comfortable with your process and understand that you are there to help them meet their needs and goals. It's your responsibility to either close the sale or close the file in a positive way.

As I've mentioned, a good indicator of strong mental and emotional toughness is taking complete responsibility for your sales successes and failures. Use your list from above as a starting point and rewrite your sales frustrations in terms of your own behavior.

"I get upset when...

- ...I don't properly qualify prospects as to their willingness to make a decision because the result is that I frequently provide proposals that get no decision."
- ...when I beg (e.g., I'll be in your neighborhood and just want to stop in to show you something) for an appointment because it frequently results in an uninterested prospect."

Commit to never blaming your prospects for your sales problems. Always recognize that the solution you are seeking is in the mirror. When you realize that you can only control yourself and you stop worrying about how your prospects act and treat you, you will be happier and more successful as a sales professional. You will also be making more trips to the bank and fewer trips to the water cooler to complain about the sale you just lost.

CHAPTER 22

From Captain
to Capitalist

E ver play a word association game? If I say "salesper-son," what words come to mind? Polyester? Slimy? Sleazy? Snake-oil? Hmmm, not very flattering.

Now, what if I say "submarine captain" (which I was, back in the day)? Commanding, impressive, fearless, leader, honor? Well, that's what people tell me when I ask them.

Then why in the world would anybody want to go from being an impressive, fearless submarine captain to being a sleazy, slimy salesperson? I did it—I loved being a submarine captain, and I love being a salesperson. But I didn't start out loving it.

What I found when I came into selling was this: Finding customers was hard, getting them to return my call was even harder, and getting them to shoot straight with me was nearly impossible. All of this was enough to make a salty old submarine captain wish he was back at sea cleaning a bilge or chasing the bad guys.

When I was running the submarine, sailors respected me, followed my orders, and told me the truth—lives depended on it. In sales, it was all different—prospects had no respect for my time; ignored my calls; didn't show up for appointments; gladly took my valuable information without paying me; controlled the agenda; and drained my energy. Once I learned to overcome these problems, I found that I loved the selling world and my role as a salesperson, and here's why.

1. **Selling pays on results.** Selling is the classic embodiment of capitalism—when I produce I am paid. I have been 100% commission from the day I got out of the Navy, and I have nobody to blame but myself when I don't get paid. I remember asking for a raise when I was a teenager; my boss said, "Your raise will become effective when you become effective." I've never forgotten that lesson. In sales, the only thing limiting my income is me; I know I'm making exactly what I'm worth—to the penny—every day.

2. **Selling solves problems and fulfills needs.** Every time I sit down with a prospective client, I am trying to help them solve a problem. If we decide to do business together, we embark on a program in which I am going to do everything I reasonably can to ensure their success. Having a client tell me that my stuff is helping them provides my greatest professional satisfaction.

3. **Selling is a psychological high.** Stand outside any factory and study the faces of the workers leaving their shift. Are you witnessing the joy of victory? No. Now, observe a salesperson who has just landed a big account, solved a customer's problem, or closed an important deal. You're watching a winner.

4. **Sales provides immediate feedback on my performance.** The reactions I get from prospects let me know how I'm doing. I've also gone back to folks who did not buy from me to ask them why. That feedback gives me a great chance to improve my skills.

The thing I liked best about being a submarine captain was having control of my own destiny. Likewise, what I like most about a selling career is that I am my own boss. Along with being my own boss, I get the chance every day to make a difference in somebody's life. These things equal true job satisfaction.

In the Navy I had a guaranteed paycheck twice a month and the benefits were great. It was a very stable lifestyle.

Security—lots of it; financial risk—none; freedom—very little. As a salesperson it's all different: There's no guaranteed income and the risk of failure is huge. But, the freedom is fantastic. The freedom to do as I please, to make as much money as I'm worth, to work when I want to and not work when I don't want to, to make a difference in peoples' lives—it's all there every day in sales.

The journey from the safe and secure life of a submarine captain to the risk-filled life of sales was rather terrifying for this old sea salt. But the destination has made it all worthwhile. That's why when people ask me, "Do you miss the Navy life?" I reply, "I loved the Navy for 18 years as the son of a submarine captain; I loved it for 28 years on active duty; and currently I love it being the father of a third-generation submarine officer—but I don't miss it. I'm having too much fun selling!"

CHAPTER 23

Make Decisions to Get Decisions

hen USAir Flight 1529 lost both engines to bird strikes just after takeoff on January 15, 2009, what do you suppose pilot Sully Sullenberger's decision process was as he opted to land in the Hudson River? Do you think he talked it over with a committee? When offered two runway options by ground controllers, do you think he said, "Let me think it over"? Do you suppose that he requested some time to do some research? It's amazing how fast you can make decisions when you have to. It's also amazing how slow you make them when you don't have to.

In his book *Blink*, author Malcolm Gladwell contends that people make their best and most accurate decisions in the first two seconds of facing a situation—in other words, in the blink of an eye. It seems inherently suspect, though, this notion that people can make correct decisions quickly. You were probably taught from an early age that haste makes waste, don't judge a book by its cover, and look before you leap. You may have been conditioned to believe that if you don't gather as much information as possible, deliberate carefully, and consider all possible options, you will end up a fool. As a result, you came to only trust your conscious, slow-paced decision processes. But, decisions made very quickly can be every bit as good as those made deliberately and cautiously. In fact, you probably remember your sixth grade teacher telling you, "Your first answer is your best answer."

No wonder prospects seem to have such difficulty making a buying decision. They're walking around with decades of head trash, bad scripts, and old tapes telling them not to trust their impulses. So they give the inevitable think-it-over answer. But is that really the problem? Is it that prospects can't make decisions, or is it that salespeople take their own slow buying cycles into their sales calls?

Think about how you buy something. If you stopped reading now and wrote down your buying process, what would it look like? Decide what I want; find it; buy it? Probably not, but that's what salespeople want prospects to do. Salespeople want prospects to make instant decisions. They don't, or they only do so slowly, and that drives sellers crazy.

In reality, salespeople themselves do the same things when they buy: procrastinate; think it over; consult with someone else (who's conveniently not present); check the budget; promise to call back next week. It's all a put off, because chances are they've made their decision in the blink of an eye but are afraid to act on it. They're either afraid to say "no" because they don't want to deal with the anticipated conflict, or they don't want to say "yes" because childhood tapes warn that they will regret it later on.

I recently spoke for an hour with Keiko, a prospect. She agreed prior to meeting to make a yes/no decision and was full speed ahead throughout our meeting. I prodded every way I could to see if she were really serious about working with me. She said she was and also that she was convinced that her return on investment would be huge.

The following conversation ensued:

Keiko: Well, I guess this is where you want a decision, but I need to think it over.

Me: No problem, Keiko, you can think it over all you want. However, since you said your biggest problem is prospects who need to think it over, it could be that it's your own decision processes that are affecting your close ratio. Chances are you've already decided not to do this with me but are having difficulty telling me. So I'm going to make it easy for both of us and close the file.

Keiko: Well, I think it would be rude of me not to let prospects think it over; it would make it seem like I'm only there for the money.

Here's my thought for Keiko (and myself when I have trouble getting people to make decisions): Success in business has a lot to do with making decisions. Good decisions, bad decisions, mediocre decisions. You have to make decisions. Once in a while you may make a bad decision, but you repair that with another, better decision and move on. Failure to make decisions leads to paralysis.

Likewise, success in sales is about getting prospects to make decisions; *yes* is a good decision; *no* is a good decision; *thinking it over* is no decision. If you are uncomfortable about making decisions, then leading people towards a decision will also feel uncomfortable. In that case, sales or business development may not be the place for you.

So, the next time you're the prospect, whatever you do, take a firm stand, look the salesperson in the eye and say "yes" or "no." Don't say you need to think it over. Either way, you'll probably be right. Sully Sullenberger made a fast decision, and he, his crew, and his passengers are alive today because he decided—in the blink of an eye.

CHAPTER 24

Cure Decision Deficit Disorder in Others

ave you ever had a problem getting started with any of the following?

- Making cold calls.
- Asking clients for referrals.
- Discussing money with a prospect.
- Following up on proposals because you're afraid the answer is going to be "no."

Even though you know these things must be done, you don't do them. Why not? You procrastinate.

Decision deficit disorder is when prospects eagerly seek your information, proposals, and advice and welcome your elaborate presentations, but then spend forever thinking it over. In other words, you find yourself dealing with prospects' procrastination. The bad news is the problem might be you, the salesperson.

Remember that there is a very strong correlation between a salesperson's own decision-making processes and what they will tolerate from a prospect. While exploring failure and risk can be helpful, these will remain intellectual exercises unless you get on with it and become more decisive. Procrastination may be part of the problem.

What are the effects of procrastination?

1. **Blocked emotional growth.** There is no status quo; you are either growing or deteriorating. Procrastination is an attempt to stand still, and that is not possible.

2. **Multiple failures.** As procrastination continues, there are no successes, just more failures. The effect is paralysis.

3. **Over-adaptation.** You don't go after your own goals; you subvert them for someone else's. For example, in a sales call, instead of saying what you want, you concede to the prospect because of fear of failure; you get caught up in the muddle of being a nice person.

The downward spiral to continued procrastination continues.

4. **Impulsiveness.** You attempt to break the cycle by becoming impulsive. But risk involves consideration of results, effects, and resources; impulse ignores these concerns. It is just a knee-jerk reaction as an attempt to do something.

When you procrastinate, you are not moving ahead with your plan. Time is moving, but you are not. Others are making progress, but you are not. Sometimes you don't even realize it. How do you identify procrastination? If the following is happening, you are procrastinating.

1. **You use the same tactic all the time.** We've all heard it: The definition of insanity is doing something the same way but expecting different results. Do you ever use a repetitive action to consistently avoid doing something?
2. **No change occurs.** You are still where you were when you started.
3. **No conclusion is reached.** Nothing is different; the same non-results occur. All you have is a nagging feeling of something unfinished.
4. **You're always waiting for something to happen.** Have you ever been sitting around hoping that a few prospects who are thinking it over would call you up and tell you they are ready to start? Most salespeople

have been there at least once. Instead of making something happen, they are waiting. Waiting means you are on somebody else's plan, not yours.

A few years ago my mother and father went shopping to buy him a winter coat. At the store, Dad walked over to the coat rack, tried on a coat, and started walking to the check out. Mom asked, "Where are you going?" Dad replied, "I'm going to pay for my new coat." Mom wanted to look further, check out other coats, go to other stores, compare prices, and make sure they were getting the best deal. Dad is a decision maker; Mom is a shopper.

What about you? Are you a decision maker or a procrastinator? Shopping is OK, but if you want to eliminate decision deficit disorder from your prospect's buying process, you need to become a more effective decision maker yourself. Simply put, this might require you to only say to salespeople selling to you the words you want to hear from your own prospects: "yes" or "no." If you don't want to be the recipient of "think-it-overs" then don't deliver such indecisiveness yourself. Understand and identify procrastination in your life and eliminate it by having a well-defined decision process.

CHAPTER 25

Collecting Psychological Trading Stamps

W hen I was a kid, many stores handed out S&H Green Stamps to customers. There were no credit card rewards points in those days. When you got home, you put your stamps in your S&H book; when it was filled, you could cash it in for a prize, like a toaster or a beach chair.

People who feel not-OK in their sales career (see Chapters 10 and 11) will likely spend time collecting psychological stamps—a counterproductive habit that can easily torpedo one's sales efforts.

Early in life people learn that expressing their true OK and not-OK feelings can cause trouble, so they learn to hide those feelings and play it safe.

One strategy people use is collecting psychological trading stamps. When something negative happens to a stamp collector, rather than appropriately expressing their emotions, they will suppress and store the negative feelings, like stamps, for later redemption.

This is known as "cashing in a book." It can take the form of some type of psychological reward, like an emotional outburst or getting drunk. In many cases the event that appears to trigger the outburst is not in proportion to the outburst; it just happened to be the final stamp, or unexpressed feeling, needed to fill the book. Since sales and business ownership can be psychologically stressful, you need to be careful to own your feelings and not collect stamps.

According to Dr. Eric Berne, psychological stamps come in colors, in accordance with the feelings they represent:

- Red stamps: anger.
- Purple stamps: hurt and abuse.
- Yellow stamps: fear.
- Gray stamps: worry about the future.
- Blue stamps: depression.
- Brown stamps: guilt.

People store and cash stamps in a variety of ways.

- Some people examine their repressed feelings when they have idle time on their hands. This can be when selling becomes too hard.
- Some people wait until they have enough stamps to justify one enormous outburst. A salesperson can be an easy target for a prospect who has a full book ready to cash in.
- Some people enjoy boasting about the size of their collection of feelings.

Healthy adults refuse to collect or trade stamps. They own their feelings in the moment whenever possible, discuss them appropriately, and then move on. The energy they save by not storing feelings can be used to promote productive interactions with others, including prospects, salespeople, managers, and subordinates.

Identify your stamp collections by recognizing the negative feelings that you get from sales at inappropriate times. For example, maybe you spent a whole afternoon making cold calls and got nowhere. Your frustration is building. Now your manager calls you and starts bugging you about setting more appointments. This would be the most likely time to cash in a book of anger stamps: "I'm sick and tired of making call after call, and now you're unhappy with me. If this is what it takes to succeed here, I quit." Or perhaps, worry stamps: "I'm a failure at this; if I don't make a sale soon I won't be able pay my rent."

Instead, try this discussion: "I don't seem to be getting anywhere with these calls. I'm feeling not-OK right now. My frustration is perhaps coming through the phone. Maybe I should resume this in the morning. Would you be willing to listen to my calls then and offer some tips on what I need to change?"

Your ultimate goal should be to eliminate all stamp collecting from your relationships. Leave stamp collecting to the philatelists. Or try collecting stamps that are green—good feeling and healthy—by performing your roles successfully. These stamps can be cashed in for a real reward like a treat after making a sale.

If you truly feel OK about yourself as well as about other people, you won't have a need to collect any stamps. Gaining greater self-awareness and dealing with your feelings in an appropriate manner will help you become more aware of the games you are playing as well as the payoffs you are seeking. You can also begin to recognize the games others try to play at your expense and refuse to play.

S&H Green Stamps was the original buyer rewards program. If you saved enough stamps and filled enough books, you could cash them in for a treat. That was a healthy program. May all your stamp collections be similarly green and healthy.

CHAPTER 26

Eliminate Your Prospect's Fears

W hen you last went shopping for a big-ticket item, were you a bit nervous? Did you have any concerns? Probably so. People usually worry, at least a little bit, that they might make a buying mistake. "Am I getting the best price?" "Are they taking me to the cleaners?" "Will my friends tell me I could have gotten a better deal?"

Fear may be the most powerful motivator affecting your buyers' decisions. However, in their effort to maintain an image of power and control, buyers will be reluctant to share their true anxieties and concerns with you. You'll increase your sales production when you help buyers discover and overcome their fears, show that you are sensitive to those issues, and then lead those buyers to the conclusion that your product will replace their fear with peace of mind.

Remember that prospects buy for their reasons, not yours. No matter how trivial you may think their fears are, they are very real to them. Here are some fears that can haunt your prospects as they go through the buying process.

- **Fear of the unknown.** People sometimes don't like what they have, but they know what they have. Many prefer the security of a painful status quo over the risk of an unknown future. In this case you need to question the prospect as to the impact of sticking with the current situation. If you can get them to state in their own words the negative effect of not making a change, they might begin to work through their fear of the unknown.

- **Fear of regret.** When you drive that brand new car off the lot, you are exhilarated and can't wait to show it to your friends. A day later, you suddenly have a sick feeling in your stomach. You hear a voice saying, "You fool, you just incurred a $400 monthly payment for something you didn't really need. Better take it back." To prevent buyer's remorse, deal with it at the time of the sale. After you've completed the paperwork, have one more conversation with your new customer. "Omar, you've just made a big decision and a big purchase. I want to make sure you're not having any doubts about the decision you made here today. Can you tell me why you decided to move ahead with this purchase?" This conversation takes guts, but you'll be amazed at how people will affirm themselves and their decisions.

- **Fear of losing self-esteem.** Everybody wants to feel OK about themselves. Setting forth this premise reminds me of an event that occurred 15 years ago: A friend laughed at me when I told him how much I had paid for a new car, and I quickly felt not-OK about myself. It was hard to enjoy my car after that. Making a wrong decision—real or perceived—can cause self-esteem to plummet.

- **Fear of relinquishing control.** Buyers want to feel in control and maintain the upper hand in the sales process. They like calling the shots and establishing the agenda. They know they have the power to delay a purchase as long as they want. If you interfere with this control, you will elevate their fear. One simple question helps: "Susan, what would you like to accomplish in our meeting today?" Asking this will go a long way toward helping your prospect feel in control right from the start.

Prospects become your customers when they believe that you are the "doctor" who can ease or eliminate their problems and fears. People feel manipulated when they're "sold" something. When it's their choice, buyers remain committed to a purchase decision.

When they conclude that they want to buy because of how they answered your questions, buyers feel ownership of their decisions and are less likely to feel foolish or regret the purchase later.

Don't let a sales call be about you, your product, or your service. Make sure it is about your prospect and solving their problems. Don't be afraid to ask prospects about their fears: "Jasmine, one of my concerns is that I might get ahead of you in this process and cause you to feel pressured. If you're feeling any pressure, please let me know immediately." Especially when there is a typical fear many prospects have when considering your product, flush it out early, such as: "Jasmine, when shopping for an auto, most people are quite concerned about getting the best deal. If that's a concern of yours, can we talk about it and what 'best deal' might look like to you?"

Deal honestly and openly with your prospect's fears in a sales call and you will eliminate many of the stalls, objections, and put-offs that can later halt the sale.

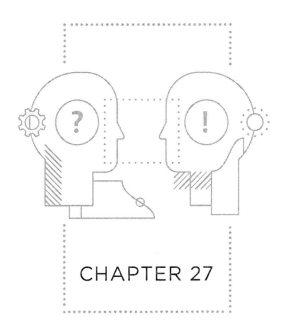

CHAPTER 27

Do You Need the Sale
or Want the Sale?

Have you ever been in front of a salesperson who appeared to be desperate for the sale? Desperate salespeople and desperate companies tend to make unnecessary concessions, cave in on price too easily, and cater to unreasonable demands from customers. Keeping a mindset of being financially independent is the first step to ensuring that you never appear desperate in front of a prospect.

The obvious problem with needing the sale in order to pay your mortgage, buy groceries, or make a car payment is that a prospect can smell that need, just as a shark smells blood. Many people tell me that they only shop for a car on the last day of the month because they believe that dealerships are feverishly trying to meet their monthly quotas and will accept smaller profits. Real estate agents say that empty houses command smaller asking prices for the obvious reason that the buyer knows the seller is desperate.

Selling is a tough business, especially when you are in your first few years and trying to establish a client base. Those who have the guts to go it on commission alone and forego the short-term security of a salary will likely face some lean months pay-wise. Combine that with the emotional ups and downs that sales puts on you and the stress of wondering if you'll be able to pay your bills this month—no wonder you might appear desperate for the sale. Nonetheless, remember this rule: No matter what your bank account looks like, your attitude in front of a prospect is this, "I'm financially independent and I don't need the business."* Another way to put it is, "Prospect Person, I believe I can help you out and I hope we end up doing business together; but if you decide against that, I'll be fine. Either way, I'm eating steak tonight."

The best way to avoid sales desperation is to keep your own financial house in order. If your commissions are particularly good one month, don't spend the extra money; take a steady draw from your bank account each month at a level

---

* Source: Sandler Selling System.

you can sustain year-round, no matter the fluctuations in your monthly commission check. Beyond that very necessary fiscal discipline, the most important thing is to create the belief and persona that you want the sale, but you don't need it.

The best movie I've seen on sales success is *Tommy Boy*—that's right, *Tommy Boy* with Chris Farley. The salvation of his family's auto parts company rests on Tommy's shoulders and his very unorthodox and rudimentary selling skills. Tommy's early sales attempts meet with dismal results. His partner Richard calls one effort, "A huge embarrassing failure." On the road, Tommy and Richard reach a point of despair as they are sitting in a country diner. Tommy orders chicken wings, but the waitress tells him that the fryers are shut down and they can have only cold items. Launching into one of his antics, Tommy convinces the waitress to start up the stove and bring him some wings. Richard, looking dumbfounded, asks Tommy, "Why can't you sell like that in front of a customer?" He replies, "What are you talking about? I was just playing around. If I don't get the wings, so what, I've still got that meat-lovers pizza in the trunk."

Did you catch that? In sales parlance, Tommy was saying, "I hope you decide to do business with me, but if you tell me 'no,' I'll be OK; after all, I'm financially independent and I don't need the business." Once Tommy did not need the sale, he was a lot more relaxed and did not appear desperate; he could just play off the "prospect's" responses and not worry about what was going to happen next. Not needing the sale enabled him to get the sale. The lesson he learned in that interaction enabled him to change his whole sales persona from desperation to confidence. He shifted from huge embarrassing failures to huge sales.

A sales call should be an Adult-to-Adult interaction where everybody comes out a winner. Groveling, begging, or otherwise appearing desperate do not lead to win-win situations. If you find yourself wanting or needing the sale more than your prospect, you're probably not going to come out a winner. Before every sales call, remind yourself, "I'm financially independent, I'd love to get this sale, but if I don't, I'll be OK; I've got a pizza in the trunk."

CHAPTER 28

TV

D o you spend more time watching TV or reading books? When markets are down, do you spend more time worrying about how you're going to sell anything or planning how you're going to beat the market? No doubt, there's plenty about which to worry, and the TV has it all—war, economy, politics; bad news, sad news, get-mad news. How is a person supposed to make a living with all this?

Start by asking yourself this question: "Who's programming my brain for success?" I decided to stop watching TV when I realized the news shows are programming for fear, failure, and a scarcity mentality. Why wouldn't they be? Keeping me scared is what keeps me tuned in—and keeping me tuned in keeps the networks' revenue coming in. Now that's some negative programming. Result: If I watch too much, I slowly and subtly buy into the idea that nobody's buying and nobody's selling. Soon I'm right there with them, not buying and not selling—just a full-fledged participant in the economic crisis. Any chance that's happening to you?

Good news: There's a cure. It all starts with belief systems—yours. Only you can program your brain for success. You choose every minute of every day whether to pump negative or positive beliefs into your sales head. If you spend time in the car with doom-and-gloom talk show hosts, constantly tune into the latest unfavorable market news, and eat dinner while watching a report on another failed company, you're planting negative seeds and creating a mindset of failure. On the other hand, you can create a positive belief system with the following activities.

- **Daily journal.** Spending 20 minutes early in the morning writing about your successes, failures, goals, and commitments to action is a tremendously powerful way to start your sales day.
- **Daily affirmations.** This is where you create positive beliefs, write them in your journal, and recite them at the start of each day. Example: "I am a selling

machine. When I sell widgets everyone benefits—
my clients, my company, my family, and me—and I
feel good." Or simply, "I am not a participant in bad
market news."

- **Weekly support group.** Form a peer accountability
  group. Find three people who are as serious about
  sales success as you are. Commit to a 40-minute conference call each week. Hold each other accountable
  for appropriate sales behaviors and activities. Provide
  encouragement and positive reinforcement.
- **Daily audio.** Turn off the radio pundits. They never
  put money in your pocket in the car. Find some
  training programs or other audio material that will
  help your sales tactics or beliefs. Turn your car into
  a classroom.
- **Daily reading.** At last count there were a few billion
  books available for reading. Some of them are good.
  But even an average book is better brain food than a
  great TV show. Turn off the TV and open a book.

Now will you immediately do all of this? Maybe not right
away. As Al Pacino said in *Scent of a Woman*, "It's too d—-
hard!" But try to do a little more each day. Negative programming is easy—because somebody else will do it for us.

If you want to take charge of programming your brain
for success, turn off the TV and start creating a positive
belief system.

CHAPTER 29

Emotional Control

H ave you ever gotten excited about the prospects of a big sale only to have it all fall apart and produce nothing in the end but disappointment for you? Becoming emotionally involved in a sales call is one of the five major conceptual roadblocks that crop up on the path to sales success. People afflicted by this tend to get excited when their prospects make promising statements, such as:

- "I really like what I see."
- "All things being equal, apples to apples, we're buying from you."

- "Call me next week; we should be ready to place an order."

I should know. I fell for every one of those during my early years in sales. In the movie *Tommy Boy*, Tommy says, "I get all excited. I'm like Jojo, the idiot circus boy with a pretty new pet. ... And that's when I blow it." It seemed like I was always fumbling the ball on the one-yard line, as if I were losing the sure sale in the last step of the close. In reality, salespeople rarely lose it in the close. Out of excitement, they spike the ball at midfield and run empty handed the rest of the way. After some promising words from a prospect, they return to the office and say, "Boss! Got one!" In reality, they "got nothing."

Developing and qualifying a potential sales opportunity takes focus, attention, resolve, and patience throughout your sales process, whatever that process is. Getting excited and emotionally involved is counterproductive. You probably would not want your brain surgeon to get emotional while operating. As I've discussed (see Chapter 23), Sully Sullenberger likely stayed unemotional as he landed his crippled USAir jet in the Hudson River. So it is best for salespeople to stay emotionally aloof when doing the job. This does not mean they are automatons. Genuine empathy, humor, compassion, and truly investing in the prospect's well-being are all required of salespeople, just as they are of the brain surgeon.

There is an actual biological impediment to remaining rational in emotionally charged situations. A human's primary physical senses enter the back of the brain through the spinal cord. From there they must travel to the front of the brain where rational thinking occurs. In order to get there, these stimuli must first pass through the limbic system, where emotional thinking occurs. In other words, people are hard wired to experience emotions first, before they respond logically to them. Remaining rational in emotionally charged situations typically takes training, experience, and practice.

In their book *Emotional Intelligence 2.0,* authors Travis Bradberry and Jean Greaves suggest that developing one's "emotional IQ" or "EQ" is equal to or of greater importance than actual IQ in determining business/sales success. They explore four strategic areas for developing one's EQ:

- Self-awareness
- Self-management
- Social awareness
- Relationship management

Let's take a brief look at the one most likely to assist in selling—self-management. After all, that's what you need to do: to manage yourself and your process when selling.

Self-management is the ability to use your awareness of your emotions to choose what you say and do. Effective self-managers ensure they are not getting in their own way and limiting their success nor frustrating others to the point of resentment. By understanding their own emotions and carefully choosing their responses, they gain power over difficult situations, react nimbly to change, and take effective steps to achieve their goals.

Here are three of the 17 recommended tactics for improving your self-management:

1. **Create an emotion vs. reason list.** When a prospect says, "Leave me your proposal; I'll be calling you next week to get started," what are your emotions telling you? What is your reason telling you? Now ask yourself. "Where are my emotions in relation to my judgment?" Leaving a proposal might solve a short-term dilemma—keeping the prospect happy. But is it in your best long-term interest?

2. **Speak with someone who is not emotionally invested in your problem.** You may not even realize that your emotions are hijacking your sales success. Seek counsel from a disinterested third party who can dissect your sales difficulties with you.

3. **Count to ten.** Thank your parents for this one. Negotiating and selling situations don't require you to respond to prospects' comments and questions in milliseconds. Take a sip of coffee, think, count in your head, and respond on your own terms. People respect a thoughtful response much more than a quick, snappy answer.

If you want to stay focused during your sales process, keep your emotions in check with effective self-management. It's OK to get excited about the prospect of a big sale—once the deal is sealed and the check clears the bank.

CHAPTER 30

Psychological Principles Sellers Need to Know

I f you are a parent with more than one child, chances are you've commented on the incredible differences in your offspring. Even identical twins show great variance in communication style, emotional makeup, thought processes, and personalities. These children grow into adults, and these adults become your buyers. Just like parents, sellers have to deal with many different personalities, each of which can challenge your interpersonal skills in a new way. You may never be a licensed psychologist, but the following list of tips may help you adapt your selling style to the prospects you meet.

1. **Everyone walks around with mental scripts written by their parents or other authority figures.** Parents and early authority figures are always around, figuratively. You may be selling to your prospect's parents as much as you're selling to that actual prospect.

2. **People do what they do because of significant emotional events that shaped their early years.** Are you aware of all the differences between traditionalists, baby boomers, Generation X, and millennials? Knowing the events that shaped people in their youth provides insight into what they believe and how they buy as adults.

3. **People are psychological "icebergs."** Many fears, prejudices, and beliefs, including those about salespeople, are unseen by others, and sometimes unknown to people themselves. Behaviors are observable; motives and fears are not.

4. **People are all pain avoiders and pleasure seekers.** Pain and pleasure are two major motivating forces of all human beings, and thus of all buyers. Use your best questioning skills to learn which is most important to your prospect and also how they define pain or pleasure.

5. **People hear what they want to hear and see what they want to see.** No two people will interpret the same event in exactly the same way. Don't assume what your prospect saw, heard, thought, or felt—ask them.

6. **People don't argue with their own data.** When you tout a feature or benefit of your product, the prospect may listen, yawn, not listen, believe you, not believe you, care, not care—and so on. But when the prospect recounts in their own words why a feature would be important to them, they're listening and they're serious. Use your questions to get the prospect to tell you why something about your product would be important to them.

7. **Everybody needs more TLC.** How important is tender loving care? Very important. Survey after survey confirms that the #1 complaint employees have about their jobs is that they don't feel appreciated. They don't hear enough praise, recognition, and commendation for the work they do. That's not just a workplace phenomenon, it's universal. Learn to genuinely and appropriately offer positive verbal strokes and compliments to your prospects.

If you want to be a great salesperson, you might think you need to read every book out there on sales tactics, methods for closing, ways to overcome objections, and more. May I suggest a different way to start? Just go to the psychology section of your favorite bookstore or library and get every book you can on human behavior and interaction.

Astute salespeople understand that in many respects they are unlicensed psychologists who just happen to be selling a product or service instead of seeing patients. No short list can provide an in-depth analysis of the intricacies and subtlety of human behavior. However, the principles above provide a solid foundation. Study them to understand your buyers better.

CHAPTER 31

Timeless Sales Lessons

I t matters not what month or year it is. Some sales lessons are timeless and might be worth revisiting on a regular basis.

Here are my top four timeless sales lessons from a recent year:

- **No more think-it-overs (TIOs).** I'd rather get a *no* than a TIO. It's embarrassing to admit that I found myself allowing TIOs. That's bad since I teach people how to eliminate TIOs! So I declared a "60-day war on TIOs." For 60 days, I journaled my sales activities and my progress in the war. Here's a sample of my journal entries: "Day 22 of my 60-day war on decision deficit disorder: Yesterday there was collateral damage. A small business owner called me and said that she wanted to get together to see if I could help her sales process. Her biggest problem: handing out lots of design plans and quotes to homeowners who then tell her they need to think it over. So I suggested that she be prepared to make a *yes/no* decision at our meeting. She said she just wanted information so that she could think it over. I told her if she could not make a buying decision at our meeting then we could never fix her problem with prospects. She canceled our meeting." As I journaled through the war, I got better and better at recognizing all the clever ways people delay in the sales process. I also realized (again) that when people are afraid to make a decision, it doesn't help matters for me to allow them to TIO. Lesson relearned: When you give your best presentation and all you get is a TIO, be gutsy enough to close the file and tell your prospect, politely, "It's over."

- **Stay off the prospect's system.** Prospects have a well-defined system for shopping. They mislead the salesperson, gather as much free information and consulting as possible, delay with some form of TIO, and then go into hiding. As soon as I give away my valuable product/company/service information without a firm commitment as to what I'll get in return, I'm on the prospect's system. Once I do that, I've lost control. My chance of a sale is close to zero. Lesson re-learned: Stay in control. Sales should be an honest, mature, Adult-to-Adult interaction. In order for it to be that, I must stay on my system, not the prospect's.

- **Sales success is all about behaviors and activities.** Nothing new there. It's just that most people in sales tend to get lazy on their prospecting activities as soon as they make a few good sales. Once you stop prospecting, the pipeline empties quickly and the commissions dry up. Do you have a personalized sales plan of required daily/weekly sales activities? Do you do what you need to do to be successful? Or do you endlessly check your email and rearrange things on your desk? Lesson re-learned: Sales success is greatly dependent on executing the right sales behaviors every day.

- **Confront your fears.** The one thing that holds most salespeople back, more than anything else, is fear: fear of rejection, fear of failure, fear of not making any money, fear of hearing "no," fear of not being liked— the list goes on and on. I re-learned that if I don't face my fears head on and deal with them, they'll paralyze me. It helps me to remember that I've learned my best sales lessons in my biggest failures. That's the consolation prize for getting a "no." Lesson re-learned: It's OK to be scared; it's not-OK to let that paralyze you.

CHAPTER 32

Thank You, Prospect Person

D o you love sales, enjoy your clients, and experience mostly positive interactions with prospects? I do. But if you've been in sales for even a short time, you know that prospects can wreak havoc on your psyche. Sales is a tough business, a contact sport, and not for the weak at heart. Even so, amidst the headaches and anxiety, prospects also teach lessons that no school could ever teach—lessons that strengthen your gut system and enable you to do better on each ensuing sales call. Below are some important lessons that prospects have taught me over the years.

Warning: These lessons sound harsh. They will only make sense to people in sales. With that caveat, I say thank you, Prospect Person, for these great lessons.

- Thank you for every think-it-over I took from you, until I got angry enough to deal with a stall that had no substance except in my own mind. You taught me to lay the ground-work for eliminating this stall early in the sales call so I don't have to deal with it after I give you my best presentation.
- Thank you for teaching me that money is a conceptual thing and not a technical thing and that you only had as much money as I was brave enough to ask for, even though that number had little to do with what you were really willing to pay for my services.
- Thank you for every time you misled me while at the same time you insisted that all salespeople were prevaricators, unethical, and dishonest. I learned that I could always be honest, up front, and open, no matter what other people are doing. But I also learned that I need to make an extra effort to be honest with salespeople when I am the prospect. How else can I expect prospects to tell me the truth?
- Thank you for every *no*, each of which made me stronger, even as I was thinking that they meant the end of

my sales career. I learned that a *no* is a decision; it's much better than a think-it-over, and it allows me to stop chasing you and move on to the next prospect.

- Thank you for not showing up for a Monday morning appointment, which had been confirmed and which I worried about all weekend. You taught me to relax and enjoy my family seven days a week.

- Thank you for using the information in my proposal to shop around town for a better deal. You taught me to stop all the unpaid consulting and to value my own time enough to give proposals only to serious customers.

- Thank you for treating me like a second-class citizen because I'm a salesperson, which crushed my self-esteem. I learned not to get my emotional needs met in sales and that my self-esteem should come from myself, my faith, my family, and my friends. Now my self-esteem is always high, no matter what happens in my sales day.

- Thank you for every time you backed out, although it left me disappointed and discouraged. I apologize for the things I thought when I saw that pink message on my desk saying, "Cancel the order; we need some time to rethink the purchase," and you wouldn't take my call or explain the change to me. You taught me to be brave enough to question you at the time of sale to make sure you would not get buyer's remorse later on.

A final thank you for putting up with my ineptness, my not OK-ness, my fears, my self-doubts, and all the other limitations I placed on myself. Only someone as tough as you could have helped me overcome all those things and become the accomplished professional salesperson I am today. Because of you I love sales, and I'll keep doing my best to help you have a better life.

For Sales Managers

....

Sales managers, the remaining chapters are geared towards growing and leading your sales team. I like to tell business owners that there are four deadly sins of sales management. They are:

- There is no sales manager.
- The owner is the sales manager.
- The best salesperson was summarily promoted to manager, based solely on excellent sales results.
- The sales manager is managing and selling, putting them in competition with the very people they're managing.

Beyond that, the most common problem in sales management is that many managers focus on managing sales results and don't see themselves as leaders of people. Effective leaders wear four hats:

- Supervisor
- Trainer
- Coach
- Mentor

As you grow and lead your sales team, perhaps these ideas will be fuel for growth, in your team as well as yourself.

CHAPTER 33

Sales Lessons for Today from Yesterday

ebruary, 1980, Winter Olympics, Lake Placid. Do you
remember the big event? A bunch of amateur hockey
players, average age 21 years old, came together as the
U.S. team and beat the USSR in the semi-finals. (Nobody
had beaten the Soviet hockey team in the Olympics in 20
years.) They then went on to win the gold against Finland in
the final. As TV commentator Al Michaels yelled at the end
of the game: "Do you believe in miracles?"

What lessons does this event have for people in sales?

(To get all the lessons, rent a copy of the movie, *Miracle*.) Consider the unbeatable Soviets as the economy in which you are all selling today. Your task is to sell more in a lousy economy than you did in a great economy—mission impossible. You're up against every obstacle imaginable—your own negative beliefs, nay-sayers, nobody has any money, nobody's spending any money. It's enough to depress anyone. But not Herb Brooks, the legendary coach of that Olympic hockey team. Herb made a plan to beat the USSR, and his plan has lessons for us today.

In a nutshell, Herb's approach seems to have been: Change beliefs to change behavior to change results. The movie *Miracle* starts with Herb telling the U.S. Amateur Hockey Association Committee that to beat the Soviets, the United States has to change the way it plays hockey. His idea is met with much disdain and heckling. Nonetheless, Herb was right. He changed the game considerably, but not without much pain and discomfort on the part of his players.

Similarly, if you want to sell in today's economy, you have to change the way you sell. That's bad news for most people because by nature people do not like to change. Whatever worked for you last year might not work today. However, it might be a case of change or die.

Start by changing your belief system. During one session when Herb shows his team some films of the Soviet team in action, he makes the following observations:

- "The main weapon of this team is intimidation. They know they're going to win."
- "Nobody has ever worked hard enough to beat the Soviets. Boys, we're going to work hard enough."
- "The NHL won't change their game, but we will." (The NHL All Stars had just lost to this Soviet team.)
- "Everybody else is afraid of these guys, but we won't be afraid of them."

Are you intimidated by the economic situation? It's hard not to be. During my Navy days I was intimidated by rough seas. But I knew that fair weather never made a good sailor. Rough seas are uncomfortable, but not unbearable. This economy is tough but not unbeatable.

Are you willing to work hard enough and change your game to adjust to the current realities? A few are; most are not. Those that do not will probably get eaten up by the economic bear. Herb's comments to his team are timely advice for those of us selling today.

One more subtle lesson in *Miracle*: Herb repeatedly takes his team to the breaking point to build up their leg muscles. He knows that the Soviets always outskate their opponents in the third period because of their superior conditioning. He tells his team over and over, "The legs feed the wolf; the legs feed the wolf."

In sales, behavior feeds the wolf. Your prospecting behavior is probably the one thing that can save you today. There's no more sitting around waiting for the phone to ring. Few salespeople really enjoy prospecting, but they always seem to be telling me, "If I could only get in front of more people, I could sell more." The person who controls how many people you get in front of looks back at you from the mirror. Want to feed the sales wolf? Do the sales behaviors.

At the end of *Miracle*, Herb says, "Three years after Lake Placid, the United States started using professional athletes in the Olympics. They called them Dream Teams. I thought it was strange that these teams never seemed to achieve the dream." You don't need to be an All Star to beat this economy. Just watch *Miracle* and heed Herb's advice to his group of amateur hockey players. They changed their beliefs, then changed their behavior, then changed the outcome. So can you.

CHAPTER 34

Recession Selling

· ·

W hat do you do during an economic downturn? Do you give in to talk of a recession? Or do you keep selling? When the economic outlook looks bad, it reminds me of the band of musicians onboard the *Titanic* playing "Nearer My God to Thee" as the ship sinks. The good news is that you don't have to go down with the ship. You have clear access to a lifeboat—your personal sales activities and behaviors.

One of my clients is the manager of a local mortgage office. If any industry sees a downturn during a recession, it is the mortgage business. This client has a saying that she tells her people: "The market will not save you." Talk about a dose of reality.

There was a time when almost anybody could make a living in the mortgage, real estate, contracting, or construction worlds. Business was rolling in; sales skills were a luxury, not a necessity. The market made a lot of people temporarily rich. Recession makes many of those overnight wonders go from feast to famine. But the only market out there is the one you create for yourself. My client tells me, "It seemed that almost daily I had to change the way I did business. I went to more events, more open houses, and more real estate offices than ever; I was on the street, meeting people, networking, and not sitting at my desk. The business was out there. I just had to work harder to get it." It was good thinking. She was adapting to a changing world.

Another client and I were recently having lunch. He owns a residential security/alarm company. For ten years, this client and his sales staff have acquired clients almost exclusively through door-to-door prospecting. At lunch I asked how the prospecting for him went when there was a downturn; he replied by showing me his fingers. He said, "These are the knuckles of a door knocker; if you ever want to know if a salesperson really knocks on a lot of doors, check for the calluses on his knuckles." He had some serious calluses.

In ten years, this client and his team have gained over 35,000 new clients by knocking on doors. Every day they head out into local neighborhoods and start knocking on doors, politely offering residents a short presentation on home security. Some of these turn into sales; many do not. Now that's a prospecting plan! How about my client's leadership? He prospected side by side with his team. He said that purchases go down slightly in a downturn. His plan of consistent daily sales behaviors, however, ensured positive sales results—in good times as well as bad.

What about you? Do you have a consistent plan of prospecting activities? Some people call that a cookbook, a list of daily, weekly, and monthly activities, such as cold calls, networking events, client calls, referral requests, and networking events, that you have identified as effective for putting you in front of prospects. The economy slows at times, but it doesn't come to a halt. People still buy, which means that somebody will always be selling. If it's not you, maybe you're waiting for the market to save you. Remember, it won't. Only that cookbook approach, a steady mix of appropriate prospecting activities along with a systematic selling system, will save you in a down economy. To achieve sales success, make sure you are adapting to a changing economy, creating your own market, and not waiting for someone else's market to save you. After all, who wants to be part of a recession?

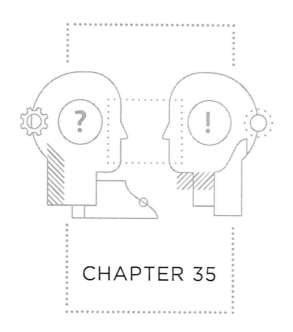

CHAPTER 35

Commission or Salary: What's Your Pleasure?

An unpleasant reality of life for salespeople is that they make exactly to the penny what they are worth. If you think you are worth more than what you are making, then why aren't you making more? You're only worth a certain amount of money if somebody is willing to pay you that much. Your concept of what you are worth along with your concept of risk and security will have a lot to do with whether you prefer to work for commission or salary.

When a business employs a sales team, each person will

achieve a different level of success and thus bring in a different amount. Any salary paid is based on the average revenue made per salesperson. The average producer gets their fair share of what they produce, but the one at the top effectively shares their cut with the one at the bottom. This would be akin to a college professor giving the whole class a C for the course and explaining to the A students that they had to share their grades with the F students. Clearly, the top performer suffers and the bottom performer benefits. Conversely, in a commission system, every producer is compensated in accordance with the classical definition of capitalism: pay on results. Top producers are paid the most and don't end up subsidizing those at the bottom of the sales charts.

One of my clients is a sales manager for a company that pays straight commission to all sales representatives. The top make $250,000/year; the average $80,000; and the bottom $30,000. This client manages a team of twenty and is responsible for recruiting new salespeople. She sees hundreds of sales resumes posted online every day. Most of them say something to the effect of "outstanding at sales," or "sales leader." When she calls these candidates, the first question they ask is, "Is this straight commission?" Once they hear the answer, they say, "Well, I'm not looking for a commission job; I'm not at that point in my career anymore." Anymore? I'm confused. You mean now that you are a super salesperson, you want to share your income with the less successful? You'd rather make $80,000 than $250,000? The truth is that straight commission tends to scare most people; they would prefer to have the perceived security of a guaranteed salary over the risk of an uncertain income.

The most ambitious, driven, and goal-oriented salespeople prefer to be on commission since that gives them the most control over their own pay and destiny. They believe that their level of achievement will be best rewarded in a commission system. The problem for owners and managers is that it is tough to find these people. The best salespeople tend to already have the best sales jobs.

Here are some tips for interviewing prospective salespeople, as far as determining their motivation: risk, entrepreneurship, and self-determination, or security, salary, and fear of failure. Does the candidate says things like:

- "What are the benefits?"
- "What's the starting salary?"
- "Is there a health plan?"

If they're talking like that, they're looking for security and are unsure of their chances of success. If they say, "The pay scale is not that important; I'll make it up in commissions," then you have a motivated player on your hands.

CHAPTER 36

Sales Culture

W hat is the sales culture in your company? Left to their own devices, would your salespeople do just enough to get by to give the illusion of being busy or to justify their base salary? Or would they go the extra mile and do whatever it takes to attain company goals and initiatives?

Most companies have salespeople in both groups. So, what distinguishes the "do whatever it takes" group from the "do enough to get by" group? The answer boils down to two things—beliefs and goals.

An individual's beliefs have more to do with their accomplishments than almost any other element. An individual with weak skills but strong beliefs about the possibility of a positive outcome will typically outperform an individual with strong skills and weak beliefs.

Why? Because people with strong beliefs will do the behavior. They believe the intended outcome can be accomplished; they will perform the necessary tasks regardless of their skill level. They may have to work harder than those with superior skills, but over time, as they continue to do the behaviors, their skills will improve.

The person with weak beliefs, despite strong skills, will at best make a half-hearted attempt at performing the tasks, or perhaps avoid doing them altogether, and instead offer several reasons why any effort would be fruitless.

Goals also drive behavior. A person with goals—personal, professional, performance, or financial—has a target at which to aim. With a target in sight, the person can develop a plan to hit it.

Here's a rule for success: Decide what you want, develop a plan, and you can bet on the outcome. The key phrase in the statement is "what you want." The goals must hold some personal meaning for you. People are generally more motivated to accomplish their own goals than they are to accomplish someone else's goals.

Combining the two concepts, you can conclude that people are most motivated to take action to pursue goals that they believe can be accomplished and also to which they have a personal connection.

As a business owner, your challenge is to provide your sales team with opportunities to channel their motivational energies in ways that support the accomplishment of company goals. An effective way to make this happen is to involve your people in goal development. It's much easier for your sales team to believe in a goal they had a part in developing. When you simply hand them a goal, it's your goal. When you collectively develop a goal, it's their goal.

"Collectively develop" doesn't mean telling your sales team on Friday to return on Monday with a plan to increase their territory sales numbers by 15%. The 15% is your number. A better strategy is to put on the table the dollar amount of the targeted increase and ask the team members to commit to how much of it will come from their respective territories. Don't be surprised if the sum of the individual commitments exceeds the total required increase.

If you really want to create a stronger sales culture, try spending as much time on your people's beliefs and goals as you do on sales tactics and techniques. Salespeople who are willing to get on board with beliefs and goals are much more likely to do whatever it takes than to do enough to get by.

CHAPTER 37

Smart Business Owners Run toward the Roar

Are you waiting out a dismal economy hoping things will get better? It might be that now is the time to grow your business.

On the plains of Africa the king of the jungle, the lion, employs an interesting tactic to catch its dinner. When a pride of lions spots a herd of something tasty, the lionesses—more nimble, more agile, and faster than the males—deploy in a semi-circle, hidden in tall grass, around one side of the herd. A male goes to the other side and lets out a roar.

The alerted herd then heads directly away from the roar—straight into the waiting lionesses. The rare animal that is wise enough to run toward the roar can normally evade the single roaring lion.

Are business owners smart enough to run to the roar?

An uncertain economy provides most businesses a painful choice: settle deeper into the hole and wait for the lionesses to start dining, or run to the roar. To muster the guts to attack this economy, consider the following advantages of doing so:

1. **Your competitors are in their own holes.** In a rough economy, most owners are more concerned with making payroll than with growing their business. Given a choice of taking a big risk to grow their company or maintaining the status quo with a perceived guarantee of keeping their job and paycheck, do you suppose most people would choose risk or safety? Getting out of the hole will put you ahead of others.

2. **Your competitor's salespeople are farming when they need to be hunting.** Often the false prosperity before a recession made selling seem easy—buyers called you, so prospecting skills dwindled and salespeople became order-takers. If salespeople pick up the phone in a recession, they may learn that their prospecting skills are outdated—as they gain those free lifetime subscriptions to their prospects' voicemail.

If your team has an active and aggressive prospecting plan, you'll be way ahead of your competition.

3. **Your competitors have slashed their marketing budgets.** A quick fix for short-term cash problems? Reducing expenses, including marketing. But what about the long haul? The one who continues to advertise even in rough times is building top-of-mind awareness in customers who will start buying again as better economic times emerge.

4. **Good people are available today as jobs are slashed to save on payroll.** Now is the time to build a great team. Few things will energize your company like the acquisition of highly capable players. Shed your C players and build your A team now.

Many businesses struggle when the market hits the skids. But it is not just the economy that does the damage. It is fear, trepidation, and a head-in-the-hole mentality.

If you want to beat the lions, come out of the hole ready to fight. Remember the words in the opening speech of the movie *Patton*: "I don't want to get any messages saying that we are holding our position. We're not holding anything." Patton's philosophy? Attack. He could as easily have said, "We're going to run to the roar."

CHAPTER 38

Winners Have Control throughout the Sale

B usiness owners, does your sales team have a winning attitude? Much has been written and said about attitude—maybe too much. But it is important. Some say, "Attitude is everything." Here's another thing, different from but related to attitude—a sense of self-accountability.

I look at this closely when assessing candidates for sales positions or when helping companies determine who on their sales team has the potential to go from good to great. Self-accountability, or self-responsibility, in the sales world refers to a person's attitude toward holding themself responsible for their results as opposed to blaming external factors such as high prices, bad leads, poor market conditions, or a lousy manager.

Recently I spoke with the owner of a local roofing company. She believed that she had the best roofing company in town. That's a good attitude. The problem was that her salespeople were constantly losing sales to the competition and thereby wasting her hard-earned leads.

I asked her what reasons they gave when they did not get the sale.

She said, "Their constant refrain is, 'Our prices are too high; they went with somebody cheaper.'"

I wondered aloud, "It sounds like their attitude is that they can only win on price. That's obviously not a battle you want to fight. Who can make a living as the lowest bidder? So they come back blaming you for their inability to close deals. What these reps are doing is not selling—it's just estimating, quoting, and then hoping for the best."

The fundamental problem was a lack of self-responsibility. It illustrates the difference between Winners and Non-Winners in sales.

In her book *Born to Win*, psychologist Muriel James states, "Although people are born to win, they are also born helpless and totally dependent on their environment. Winners successfully make the transition from helplessness to independence to interdependence. Non-Winners do not.

Somewhere along the way they begin to avoid being responsible for their own lives."

In sales, Winners take full responsibility for whatever happens. With every *no*, they learn a lesson and are constantly working to improve their sales behaviors, attitudes, and techniques. Non-Winners explain poor results with complaints and "if onlys," including:

- "If only the owner would advertise more."
- "If only we had better leads."
- "If only our prices were lower."

Winners do not play helpless nor do they pass blame. Winners are accountable for their own lives; they are their own bosses, and they know it. That doesn't mean Winners won't submit to or respect authority. It means they will always look in the mirror when trying to solve their sales problems. For example, a Non-Winner will complain, "I hate it when prospects tell me they want to think it over. Why can't they make up their minds?" A Winner understands that they have control in a sales call, if they choose to take it, and can set the conditions from the start that will help a prospect make a *yes* or *no* decision. If a Winner gets a think-it-over, they look inside and say, "I need to do a better job of uncovering my prospect's decision-making process before I give all my information away, and I need to set the conditions for a decision and eliminate the possibility of a think-it-over. I can and will do better next time."

Non-Winners may lament they are not getting in front of enough people because their company does not advertise enough—as if to say, "Marketing is not my job; my job is to sell." Winners don't wait for leads to come to them. They have a well-defined prospecting plan and go out to find their own customers. They know that waiting for leads won't feed their family, so a Winner adopts an attitude that says, "Creating customers is my job—from prospecting to selling to servicing." Now there's a person who's taking responsibility for their own success.

Attitude is important in sales—but attitude is more than just being upbeat and excited. When you're looking to hire new salespeople, make sure you hire Winners who are willing to take full responsibility for their results. That attitude will take you and them to the bank.

CHAPTER 39

Can Sell or Will Sell?

Do you have people on your sales team who should be selling more but something always seems to be holding them back? This is not unusual; there are a lot of salespeople who never perform up to their potential. Typically the solution is to send them to a one-day sales seminar to get them motivated or else have the sales manager spend a few days making calls with them and teaching them better techniques. These corrective tactics rarely have any long-term effect. Here's why.

The first group of people who don't sell well are those

who can sell but won't. These people are lacking in one or more of four critical competencies: ambition, drive, outlook, and accountability. Some refer to these simply as "fire in the belly." People who are lacking in this area can learn all the right techniques and get pumped up at a seminar. But the problem is that selling is hard, much harder than it looks, and people without ambition and drive will give up when the going gets tough. Motivation must come from within if it is going to last; the motivation obtained at a short-term seminar usually wears off within a day. People lacking in accountability will always blame external factors for their poor sales performance and be reluctant to point the finger at the only thing they can fix—themselves. If you have people like this on your sales team, the best thing you can do with them is to get them off the bus; let them go work for your competition. There's really no fixing them. Motivational training does not work. Critical core competencies can only be improved by change from within.

There's another group of marginal sellers; these people do have hope. These are people who will sell but can't. They are internally motivated and have the right attitudes and sense of self-responsibility necessary to sell well. However, even with training in the right techniques, they still can't execute because they have a conceptual problem that limits their ability to perform a given technique in a sales situation. Some examples of such problems are: weak money concept, high need for approval, fear of rejection, or trying to get one's emotional needs met in a sales call. These performance problems can be corrected, but first let's see how they interfere with sales success.

Take, for instance, people with a high need for approval. When faced with an uncomfortable situation in selling such as asking for money, these people will worry more about the prospect's opinions and happiness than about getting the sale. They will typically assume that asking for money is going to upset the prospect. You can teach them all the right techniques and words to use to ask for money. But, when faced with a perceived choice of keeping a prospect happy versus leaving a sales call with a check, they'll choose the former over the latter. If you want to see where your people stand on need for approval, just ask them this question: "What's most important in a sales call—preserving the relationship or closing the sale?" You'll get a lot of well-founded and well-intentioned debate. But the truth is that people who vote for preserving the relationship typically have a need for approval that can interfere with their sales efforts. (I've had a few business owners and managers tell me that I am wrong and that selling is about creating relationships. I always wonder why their performance charts show how many sales were made last month and not how many relationships were created.)

Many conceptual selling problems, such as a high need for approval, can be corrected. However, a one-day seminar won't do it. These problems require a change in belief systems. This takes repeated exposure in an ongoing effort (as discussed in Chapter 20) that will, over time, instill new, positive beliefs about the seller's ability to execute effective selling techniques. Also, the seller needs lots of opportunities to practice, and fail, in front of real-life prospects. Each failure can be a learning, albeit frustrating, experience in which a seller with the proper drive, ambition, and attitude resolves to become the person who can sell and will sell.

CHAPTER 40

Sell Yourself before Selling Others

Sales managers: Have you ever had a salesperson who was full of ambition and drive, had a positive outlook about selling, and also possessed a great sense of self-responsibility, and yet, could not "pull the trigger" on the big deals? They might have great technique and excellent product knowledge, but something still holds them back. This person may have a conceptual problem with selling, and all the technique training in the world won't fix it. Be on the lookout for the most common conceptual selling problems, which are listed below.

1. **Need for approval:** Everyone wants to be liked; salespeople are no different. Despite what the buying public thinks, salespeople have feelings and truly want to please their customers. Frequently this desire for approval causes a salesperson to worry more about being liked than about getting a check and closing the sale. As discussed in Chapter 39, being liked is fine and relationships are important, but make sure your people know that relationships are opened when sales are closed.

2. **Money concept:** A salesperson recently confided in me, "I'm intimidated by wealth." She had grown up with little money and, at an annual pay of about $52K, she was out-earning everybody in her extended family. The result was a weak money concept, causing her to believe it when a prospect says, "Your price is too high." The first discount a sales representative makes is usually in their head. It goes like this: "The prospect is right; our price is too high. If I want to get the sale, I need to lower the price. I'll just take a smaller commission." Prospects will always try to make the sale about price. A salesperson with a strong money concept will not allow that to happen.

3. **Emotions:** Sales is an emotional business. Prospects

are fickle and frustrating, and it's part of their plan to keep you wondering if and when you'll get the business. As soon as a salesperson becomes emotionally involved in a sales call, they will begin to lose objectivity and control. As you know, sales is no place to get your emotional needs met; sales is for going to the bank.

4. **Behaviors:** There is a very strong correlation between a salesperson's own buying habits and what they will tolerate from their prospects. If your salespeople are accepting a lot of think-it-overs (TIOs), chances are they are slow decision makers themselves. The salesperson who told me she was intimidated by wealth was also getting a lot of TIOs. I asked her about the last large purchase she made. It was a new auto; it took her six weeks and four conversations with the salesman from first look to purchase. She told me that when her own prospects want to TIO, it makes absolute sense to her—no wonder. When salespeople strengthen their own decision-making processes and buying behaviors, they become better at leading their prospects towards decisions as well.

Conceptual selling problems are harder to detect than product knowledge or technique deficiencies. They can be fixed, but the cure is not simple or quick. It takes recognition and acknowledgment of the problems, adoption and implementation of new belief systems, and constant reinforcement and encouragement from management. With conceptual roadblocks removed, average salespeople can become superstars.

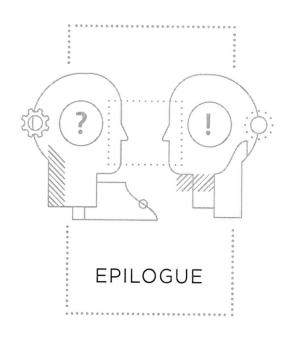

EPILOGUE

Fears, anxieties, emotional trading stamps, psycho-logical games, failure, procrastination, change or die, life scripts, head trash, not-OK—goodness! If I had known all this was part of sales, I might never have embarked on the journey. One of my Navy mentors used to say, "Fore-warned is forearmed." I was not forewarned. It's likely that you weren't either. But now that we're both in sales, the more we know about the mental challenges involved, the better we will be equipped to deal with them.

There are many sales training programs available today

and many effective selling systems. The advantage for me and so many others of discovering Sandler Training was that it deals with the psychological challenges of sales as well as the tactical and intellectual processes necessary to be a consistent and top sales producer.

Here's the point I want to leave with you. Reading a book about sales challenges is a start, but for most, attempting to create lasting change it is not enough.

Journeys take time, effort, and engagement; reinforcement is the key. Having a relationship with a mentor, a coach, or an accountability group is a necessary aspect of that reinforcement. Also, time is required to learn and sustain new habits and processes, such as:

- Growing your Adult as the executive of your personality.
- Being OK being not-OK.
- Being a better decision maker.
- Eliminating procrastination.
- Overcoming fears such as discussing or asking for money.
- Breaking through your comfort zone.
- Improving your self-image.
- Becoming a more courageous you.

If you would like to consider pursuing some of these processes, if you want to improve your outlook on your sales career, or if you are wondering if your sales team could benefit from a fresh approach, I suggest looking up your local Sandler Training office (at www.sandler.com). Call them to chat about your sales career/professional situation. Tell that Sandler trainer/coach about your goals, ambitions, and dreams, and see if they inspire you enough to take them on your journey. If not, just say, "No, thanks!" If so, then say, "Sign me up!" But whatever you do, don't procrastinate. Don't say, "I need to think it over." Take action. Visit www.sandler.com.

Look for these other books on shop.sandler.com:

SALES SERIES
Asking Questions the Sandler Way
Bootstrap Selling the Sandler Way
Call Center Success the Sandler Way
Digital Prospecting
The Contrarian Salesperson
LinkedIn the Sandler Way
Prospect the Sandler Way
Sandler Enterprise Selling
The Sandler Rules
The Unapologetic Saleswoman
Why People Buy
You Can't Teach a Kid to Ride a Bike at a Seminar

MANAGEMENT SERIES
Change the Sandler Way
Customer Service the Sandler Way
Lead When You Dance
Motivational Management the Sandler Way
The Right Hire
The Road to Excellence
The Sales Coach's Playbook
The Sandler Rules for Sales Leaders
The Success Cadence
Transforming Leaders the Sandler Way
Winning from Failing

MOTIVATIONAL SERIES
Accountability the Sandler Way
From the Board Room to the Living Room
Sandler Success Principles
Succeed the Sandler Way

INDUSTRY SERIES
Making Channel Sales Work
Patient Care the Sandler Way
Selling in Manufacturing and Logistics
Selling Professional Services the Sandler Way
Selling to Homeowners the Sandler Way
Selling Technology the Sandler Way

 Sandler Training

The Sandler Selling System®
MICROLEARNING COLLECTION

Are you or your sales team...

- Too pushy, or worse, too wimpy on sales calls?
- Losing momentum and sales you know you deserve?
- Making it up as you go along and hoping for the best?

The Sandler® Microlearning Collection will show you how to:

- Develop a prospecting plan that generates more referrals.
- Take control of the sales process and close more sales.
- Overcome common negotiation tactics and create win-win outcomes.

Think like a professional and use a proven system to learn new sales skills.

Enroll today!
sandler.com/sellingsystem